THE NORTH
DOWNS WAY

ABOUT THE AUTHOR

KEV REYNOLDS, author of this guide, is a freelance writer, photo-journalist and lecturer who lives in the Kent countryside when not trekking or climbing in distant mountain regions. A prolific compiler of guidebooks, his first title for Cicerone Press appeared in 1978 (*Walks & Climbs in the Pyrenees* – now in its 4th edition); this is his 26th book for the same publisher, with others being researched at present. A member of the Alpine Club, Austrian Alpine Club and Outdoor Writers' Guild, his passion for mountains in particular and the countryside in general remains undiminished after 40 years of activity, and he regularly travels throughout Britain to share that enthusiasm through his lectures. Organisations wishing to book Kev for a lecture should write to him c/o Cicerone Press Ltd, 2 Police Square, Milnthorpe, Cumbria LA7 7PY.

Advice to Readers

Readers are advised that while every effort is taken by the author to ensure the accuracy of this guidebook, changes can occur which may affect the contents. It is advisable to check locally on transport, accommodation, shops, etc, but even rights of way can be altered.

The publisher would welcome notes of any such changes.

THE NORTH DOWNS WAY

by

Kev Reynolds

CICERONE PRESS
2 POLICE SQUARE, MILNTHORPE, CUMBRIA LA7 7PY
www.cicerone.co.uk

© Kev Reynolds 2001
ISBN 1 85284 316 0

A catalogue record for this book is available from the British Library.

Cicerone guidebooks by the same author

Front cover: *Beyond Wrotham the way leads through Trosley Country Park (Section 6)*

CONTENTS

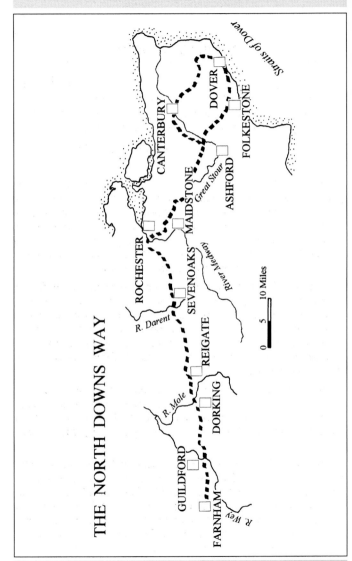

THE NORTH DOWNS WAY

INTRODUCTION

'The soul of a journey is liberty, perfect liberty, to think, feel, do just as one pleases… Give me the clear blue sky over my head, and the green turf beneath my feet, a winding road before me, and a three hours' march to dinner – and then to thinking!'

William Hazlitt (1778–1830)

I'm one with Hazlitt, when it comes to long distance walks. Except, perhaps, my preference would be for an eight or nine hour march to dinner, rather than just three. Spread the day thinly, I say; set out soon after breakfast with a cheese roll and an apple in the rucksack and dismiss from mind any thought of the next night's rest – and simply wander. Let the trail ahead guide your feet, leaving each of the senses free to absorb whatever the countryside has in store.

Walking the North Downs Way provides ample scope for the liberty to think, feel, do just as you please. Mostly the trail is clear, waymarking adequate, the spacious Downs edging a far horizon as they make that long, generous arc round the low-lying Weald, so that there are few (if any) demands to check the map or compass, and you can free the mind to drift with the clouds. Others have done just that, for generations.

'From the Straits of Dover to Farnham,' said Hilaire Belloc, 'Nature herself laid down the platform of a perfectly defined ridge, from which a man going west could hardly deviate, even if there were no path to guide him.' And we, going east, could hardly disagree.

The North Downs have acted as a highway since before Neolithic times. Since the Wealden forest was too dense and tangled to allow easy access, the high and broad-backed downland gave an opportunity to hunt, to travel, or to drive livestock from one pasture to another, and (much later) from pasture to market. Drove roads gave way to green lanes, while some of the footpaths and trackways adopted by the North Downs Way in the 21st century may well have

The trail is flanked by silver birch trees on the way to Ranmore Common (Section 2)

been stamped out long before the Romans came to these shores. Now there's food for thought...

Today the line of the downland scarp is traced by motorways and a high speed railway, and nothing can better underscore the frenetic nature of modern living than to view in the distance the haste of wheeled traffic while you stroll across a rabbit-cropped meadow, birds singing from a nearby spinney, as you let the hours drift slowly by. Walking day after day for a hundred miles and more is the perfect antidote to the stresses of workaday life; it's a means of getting life in perspective. And along the North Downs Way you can learn something of our ancestry, learn from the past and balance those lessons with the present.

The North Downs Way

The North Downs Way National Trail offers the walker a very different experience from that on the South Downs Way, for while the SDW challenges with some steepish ascents and descents, the NDW is much more gentle with fewer climbs, and where these are made, the gradients are generally much less demanding. There's more habitation along the North Downs Way but, surprisingly in view of the proximity of major centres of commerce and industry, and large residential areas (especially between Farnham and Detling), you meet far fewer walkers. Even in mid-summer it's perfectly possible to wander the trail for long periods in splendid isolation.

The North Downs are more heavily wooded than their counterpart on the south side of the Weald, but when the Way bursts out of the woods there's often a surprise view to stop you in your tracks, the revelation of patterned field and meadow, or orchard, vineyard or hop garden spread below as if to underline the fact that the Downs form a backing in places to the 'Garden of England'.

That garden is explored in detail on a spur to Canterbury, while the direct route to Dover excites with the famous White Cliffs plunging to the surf hundreds of feet below the footpath.

There are many historic sites along the Way. There are several Neolithic burial chambers, Roman roads, charming villages and tiny hamlets, England's premier cathedral city and its busiest ferry port. There are bold stone castles and country cottages trim with thatch.

There are streams and rivers, ponds and lakes that catch the sun and dazzle its light, that attract wildlife and a rich diversity of plantlife too – anyone interested in natural history will have a field day. And, of course, there are the contrasts of landscape that enrich each day's walk and make a journey along the North Downs Way a truly memorable experience.

As the above quotation from Belloc suggests, the route could be tackled from Dover round to Farnham, but the journey described in this guide takes the opposite view, preferring instead to walk eastwards, as would the pilgrim. So for the sake of our modern-day pilgrim the National Trail, which was officially opened in September 1978, begins in Farnham and ends in Dover. At Boughton Lees near Wye the route forks; one stem heading north to Canterbury, while the main route continues through Wye and follows the escarpment to the outskirts of Folkestone, then on to Dover by way of a breezy path over Shakespeare Cliff. The direct route to Dover measures roughly 123 miles (198km), while the Canterbury loop is about 130 miles (208km) long, and for most of its course between Farnham and Canterbury, it either coincides with, or parallels, the older Pilgrims Way.

For the first 14 miles (22km) out of Farnham the route traverses a range of sandy hills to the south of the Downs, but after crossing the lovely viewpoint of St Martha's Hill east of Guildford, it then strikes north to the chalk crest of Albury Downs at Newlands Corner. From then on the North Downs Way remains true to its name and largely traces the southern escarpment on a series of footpaths, tracks and brief stretches of quiet country lane as the North Downs spread east and south-east across Surrey and Kent before being abruptly cut by the English Channel.

In four places the downland wall has been breached by river valleys. In Surrey it is the River Mole below Box Hill which causes the first breach. In Kent it is the Darent at Otford, the Medway at Rochester and Great Stour near Wye that have broken through the lofty chalk barrier to create valleys whose characteristics are all very different from one another. The Mole's is a comparatively narrow valley, a wooded slice with Dorking to the south and Leatherhead to the north. The Darent Gap north of Sevenoaks is a much more open swathe, the low-lying water-meadows beside the innocent stream teasing with prospects of gentle walks for other days. The most profound breach is that caused by Kent's major river, the navigable Medway, tidal as far as Allington near Maidstone. Where the Medway has muscled its way through the Downs, the valley has been industrialised, although the trail of the North Downs Way barely has a glimpse of this before crossing high above the river on the M2 motorway bridge. Contrast this with the Great Stour whose valley breaks the downland wall between Wye and Canterbury, a rural backwater of splendid tranquillity and long views.

Between Farnham and Guildford the trail remains low, weaving across farmland interspersed with woods, coming now and then to a patch of heath from which the Hog's Back is seen to the north. The Ordnance Survey map shows major highways scoring through the country nearby, yet walkers on the North Downs Way are largely ignorant of unseen (and mostly unheard) traffic on those roads. In springtime bluebells make a haze of blue on the woodland edge, in summer foxgloves stand sentry beside the trail, and in early September ripe bilberries tempt among the heathlands.

The River Wey interrupts the line of the walk on the outskirts of Guildford, shortly before the path joins that of the Pilgrims Way leading onto St Martha's Hill, crowned by a flint-walled church at 573ft (175m) above sea-level. Though of modest altitude (on paper, that is) St Martha's offers the first of many awe-inspiring views across the heavily wooded Weald, but it is here that the route deserts both the Pilgrims Way and the sand hills, turning north to cross a shallow valley then slanting up to Newlands Corner on Albury Downs and the walk's first true chalk downland.

For some distance east of Newlands Corner the trail pushes through woodland, breaking out here and there to cropped grass and orchids, and surprise views south to Leith Hill and an extensive ridge of greensand beyond which lies the Weald. Then, having crossed Ranmore Common, the route skirts a large vineyard as it descends into the Mole Valley. Here the river is crossed on romantic stepping stones, followed by a sharp ascent of much-loved Box Hill. This signals the start of a roller-coaster section, dodging in and out of woodland interspersed with open panoramic highpoints, one of the best being between Colley Hill and Reigate Hill.

Between Reigate Hill and Ockley Hill a plague of motorways and railway lines threatens to disrupt the onward route, but the North Downs Way planners have successfully negotiated a way across with very little tarmac underfoot, and soon after leaving Merstham the crest of the Downs is regained once more, where the Pilgrims Way carries the journey over agricultural land for a while. Above Oxted the unmarked line of the Greenwich Meridian is crossed, and between here and Westerham Hill the trail exchanges Surrey for Kent. Where the county boundary is met, a special marker stone announces that you've walked 48 miles since Farnham, but have another 65 miles to walk to Canterbury, and 77 to Dover.

Briefly beyond Westerham Hill a hint is given of high-rise buildings on the outskirts of London – a reminder that the city is half a day's walk away. But you quickly shun this by dodging back into woodland, and when the path re-emerges it is to see the Darent Gap looming. Before tackling this, graceful Chevening House, official country residence of the Foreign Secretary, is seen slumbering below at the foot of the Downs.

Across the Darent Valley at Otford another sharp climb returns the trail to the downland crest for a section that mostly keeps to the scarp edge – with all the visual delights that entails – before making a sudden descent to the Pilgrims Way which, since Otford, has been restricted to a narrow metalled lane. Where the North Downs Way joins it, however, this becomes a track, then footpath, leading to Wrotham. Trosley Country Park is next and, thanks to its great popularity, it is whilst walking through it that you're likely to lose any sense of solitude – though this is short-lived.

Out of the Country Park a sunken track takes you down to the Pilgrims Way yet again, joining it just a short stroll away from one of the Neolithic burial sites that form part of what has become known as the Medway Culture. The Pilgrims Way is followed eastward for only a mile before returning up the scarp slope at Holly Hill, then plunging into an extensive woodland section above the Medway Valley.

Crossing the Medway on a motorway bridge in view of Rochester's castle and cathedral is at once exhilarating and hideous! Exhilarating because you're high above the river and with long prospects downstream with the Downs arcing blue into the distance; hideous on account of the heavy traffic thundering past, forcing you to muse on the madness of speed and its effect on the environment. Thank heaven that crossing is soon over!

Over Wouldham Common sanity is restored on an undemanding walk to Blue Bell Hill, then it's down to Kits Coty House, the giant upright stones of another Neolithic burial chamber standing on a downland slope with far-reaching views across the Medway Valley.

East of Kits Coty a long stretch with few distant views delivers the North Downs Way to Detling Hill, beyond which a sudden return to open country shows the vast expanse of the eastern Weald spread below. The trail tucks round the outline of Thurnham Castle, slopes down to rejoin the Pilgrims Way at Hollingbourne, and follows that gentle route for many miles above Harrietsham and Lenham, only just missing Charing – a village well worth making a short diversion to visit. But from there until you reach Boughton Lees, you lose any meaningful association with the Downs – despite the fact that you're actually on them. However, there are compensations, one of which is the crossing of Eastwell Park and an opportunity to look at the remains of St Mary's Church on the north shore of Eastwell Lake.

With the North Downs Way dividing outside Boughton Lees the continuing eastward option enters Wye, a lovely small town noted for its agricultural college, then climbs onto the downland crest for one of the finest sections of the whole walk. This hugs the scarp edge for a while across Wye Downs and Broad Downs, then deserts it in order to pass through Stowting. But soon after, another glorious stretch is encountered which takes the walk above Postling (where Joseph Conrad once lived), descends to Etchinghill, then up again to wind round the steep upper scarp above the gruesome marshalling yards of the Channel Tunnel Terminal. Ignoring this blot on the landscape the trail makes a loop round ancient Castle Hill, site of a 12th century Ring and Bailey castle, before setting out on the final clifftop march that leads over Shakespeare Cliff and ends in Dover itself.

The northern spur option from Boughton Lees visits Chilham, one of Kent's most attractive villages, then to Old Wives Lees, passing through acre after acre of orchard country on the way to Canterbury.

Chilham, near Canterbury, is one of Kent's most attractive villages (Section 10a)

The architectural glories here are enough to tempt a delay, but pushing on takes the walk to Patrixbourne (whose church demands a brief visit), then across Barham Downs to Womenswold in the back country, continuing then through pleasant but un-downlike agricultural landscapes to reach Shepherdswell. From here a final eight mile walk makes an exploration of gentle East Kent farmland that culminates with a remarkably easy entry into Dover, whose castle overlooks the town from a prominent site that has been fortified for nearly two thousand years.

Accommodation

A wide range of accommodation is available throughout the North Downs Way, ranging through campsites, youth hostels, private b&b, country pubs and high-priced hotels. On each section of the walk described in this guide I have indicated where, *at the time of research*, such accommodation could be found. Anyone planning to tackle the North Downs Way end to end is advised to obtain a copy of the *North*

Downs Way Practical Handbook, an invaluable, regularly updated publication which lists the great majority of accommodation and refreshment facilities along or near the route. The *Handbook* is published by, and available from, the Strategic Planning Directorate at Kent County Council – see Appendix A.

Another annually updated source of recommended accommodation along the North Downs Way (and South Downs Way) is the *Ramblers' Yearbook and Accommodation Guide* which is sent free of charge to all members of the Ramblers' Association – see Appendix A.

At the time of writing the YHA has four hostels on or near the route. These are at Tanners Hatch (Section 2), Kemsing (Section 5), Canterbury (Section 10a) and Dover (Sections 11 & 12a). Advanced booking is advised, especially during school holidays and at weekends. Full details of addresses, facilities and telephone numbers are given in the YHA Guide which comes free with membership – see Appendix A for the YHA National Office.

Stilwell's National Trail Companion is another useful annual directory which lists sources of accommodation along dozens of long distance footpaths in Britain, including of course both the North and South Downs Ways. If unavailable from your local bookshop, contact Stilwell Publishing – see Appendix A.

Practical Advice

As a National Trail, managed jointly by Surrey and Kent County Councils with support from the Countryside Agency (formerly Countryside Commission), the North Downs Way is adequately waymarked with arrows bearing an acorn symbol, and is well maintained and checked for obstructions. Walkers may therefore expect reasonable conditions along the whole route. However, although it follows a series of defined rights of way, some sections are on bridleways shared with cyclists and horse riders and can be very muddy in inclement weather, while in other places the route travels along byways used by motorised traffic where extra care should be taken.

Colour-coded waymarks clarify the right of use of these various designations: yellow arrows indicate footpaths (walkers only); blue

On Oxted Downs the way cuts round the flank of the hills
(Section 4)

arrows show a bridleway (walkers, cyclists and horse riders); red arrows indicate a byway (all traffic).

Whether you plan to walk the whole route end to end, or pick out isolated sections for day walks, some consideration should be given to conditions underfoot. Comfortable, well-fitting and weatherproof footwear is essential to the enjoyment of the walk, for you need to be prepared for all weathers at all times of the year. In summer no less than winter, rain and wind can make you very cold, especially when walking across open downland, so clothing should take account of this. Warm and waterproof outer garments ought to be carried or worn on every stage of the long walk. On the other hand, in summer don't forget the effects of too much sun – so include a brimmed hat to protect head and neck, and use suncream too. A basic first aid kit to deal with cuts, scratches and blisters can to be carried in the rucksack, together with food for the day, some form of liquid refreshment, and Ordnance Survey maps for the area. Although a compass is not essential, one could be helpful in the unlikely event of your getting lost – as long as you know how to use it, that is.

Should you intend to stop for refreshment in pubs or cafés along the way, please be considerate to the patrons and either remove your boots or cover them with plastic bags to avoid leaving a trail of mud behind you.

Although no indication of timing is given for any stage of the route, walkers should assume an average of 2½ miles per hour. When trying to estimate how long it will take to get from A to B, do not forget to make allowances for refreshment stops, photographic delays, and time taken to consult the map or guidebook. These are likely to add considerably to your total walking time. Remember too that in hot, wet or windy conditions you will inevitably take longer, and if there are any ploughed fields to cross your pace will be much slower.

Getting There – and Back

Farnham and Dover are both served by rail from London: Farnham services come from Waterloo, Dover's from London Victoria. A good many other country stations are located near enough to the North Downs Way to give reasonably easy access, and these will be especially useful for anyone planning to tackle the route in day stages.

In Surrey these stations are Guildford, Shalford, Chilworth, Gomshall, Dorking, Deepdene, Westhumble, Betchworth, Reigate, Merstham, and Oxted. In Kent they are at Otford, Kemsing, Borough Green, Halling, Cuxton, Eyhorne Street (Hollingbourne), Harriets-ham, Lenham, Charing, Wye, Chilham, Chartham, Canterbury, Bekesbourne, and Shepherdswell.

Appendix B lists telephone numbers for timetable and train route information. For details of local bus services in the North Downs 'corridor' please refer to the individual County Public Transport Groups, also listed in Appendix B.

Using the Guide

For the purposes of this guide the route has been broken into 11 stages to cover the main walk from Farnham to Dover, with three

Milestone on the trail to Wrotham (Section 5)

additional stages for the northern spur via Canterbury. The shortest of these is just 7½ miles (12km), the longest 13¾ miles (22km), but since there's the possibility of finding accommodation at various intermediate points, it's not essential to stick to the itinerary set out here, and walkers can either lengthen or shorten most stages to suit.

As mentioned above, the precise location of accommodation and refreshment facilities is not given, but a rough indication has been made to ease advanced planning. Where a bracketed distance, ie (+½ mile), is given in the fact panel, this shows that accommodation or refreshments can be found half a mile off the route. A light dotted line on the relevant sketch map also shows where that route diverges from the main North Downs Way, while the text clearly indicates these diversions.

Sketch maps that accompany the text are given as a rough guide only, to show the line of the route and to help plot the way on other maps. Of these the Ordnance Survey 1:50,000 scale (1¼" = 1 mile) Landranger series should be adequate, although the newer 1:25,000 (2½" = 1 mile) Explorer series gives much greater detail and has the line of the North Downs Way clearly marked. No fewer than eight sheets of Explorer maps would be required for the whole route, or six of the Landranger series to cover the same distance. Also available are two Harveys maps at a scale of 1:40,000 (a little over 1½" = 1 mile) covering the route: the *North Downs Way West* (185 137 367 5; £8.95), covering Farnham to the Medway, and the *North Downs Way East* (185 137 379 9; £8.95), covering Dover to the Medway. The relevant maps are noted in the fact panels for each walk stage. Placenames marked on the sketch maps are emboldened in the text to aid orientation.

Wherever the route passes, or views from a distance, a particular place or feature of interest, this is marked in the text with an identifying number, viz [1]. At the end of the route description a corresponding number carries a brief outline of information for that feature.

Should you find the route unaccountably obstructed, or have difficulty due to lost or vandalised waymarks at awkward junctions, you should write with details to the North Downs Way Manager, or Rights of Way Officers of the responsible County Council (see Appendix A). However, if you find the route has been altered in any meaningful way, and the descriptions in this guide no longer apply, I'd very much appreciate a note to this effect. A postcard sent to me via the publisher will be gratefully received, and details will be checked in advance of any new printing or revised edition of this book.

And finally, please treat the countryside with the care and respect it both deserves and needs:

- Guard against all risk of fire
- Fasten all gates
- Keep dogs under control
- Keep to public paths across farmland, and avoid taking short cuts which cause erosion
- Use gates and stiles to cross fences, hedges and walls
- Leave livestock, crops and machinery alone
- Take your litter home
- Help to keep all water clean
- Protect wildlife, plants and trees
- Take special care on country roads
- Make no unnecessary noise.

SECTION 1: FARNHAM TO GUILDFORD

Distance:	**11 miles (17½km)**
Maps:	**Harveys North Downs Way West 1:40,000**
	OS Landranger 186 Aldershot & Guildford 1:50,000
	OS Explorer 145 Guildford & Farnham 1:25,000
Accommodation:	**Farnham, Guildford**
Refreshments:	**Farnham, Puttenham, Compton, Guildford**

'The soil is good; the houses are neat; the people are neat; the hills, the woods, the meadows all are beautiful.' So said the much-travelled William Cobbett of the area covered by this stage of the North Downs Way. Cobbett (1763–1835) was born in Farnham in what is now the pub named after him, and although he walked nowhere unless it was impossible to ride, he had an unchallenged intimacy with the Downs and the Weald that adds weight to his words. Nearly two centuries on they remain largely true.

Despite the fact that this initial stage of the long walk gives no real flavour of the Downs, it makes a fine introduction with an abundance of wild flowers in the meadows, banks and hedgerows, and plenty of wildlife too. The walking is not too demanding, with no major ascents or descents to tackle – these will come later – and the way is mostly so well defined that it's possible to wander for mile upon mile without more than a casual reference to the map. In the place of open downland, this western end of the route offers a series of gentle agricultural landscapes, punctuated with woodland and one or two sandy heaths. The River Wey is met at the start and the finish, but in between there are few other streams and no lakes or ponds of note. The route passes through only one

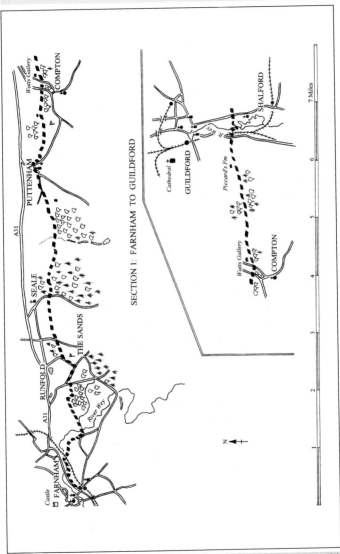

SECTION 1: FARNHAM TO GUILDFORD

village and for long stretches there will be little habitation visible. However, study of the map will show that you are never very far from a farm, road or a group of houses, even if these are not visibly evident from the footpath.

Close to the Surrey/Hampshire border, **Farnham**[1] marks the official start of the North Downs Way with a noticeboard and a carved post set beside a busy junction on the A31 a little west of the town's railway station. From the station walk downhill to the traffic lights (Grid ref: 844466) and turn right. A tarmac footpath soon brings you to a narrow lane where you bear right. The lane is flanked by trees, and at a T-junction you turn right again on another metalled lane which becomes a pitted drive running alongside the River Wey,[2] here a reedy, rather unimposing – but nonetheless pleasant – stream. At the entrance to The Kiln turn right to pass through a brick railway arch, where a footpath continues ahead between woodland and meadows. Across the meadows to the left High Mill House can be seen.

At a junction of paths the North Downs Way veers left, shortly after which you cross a stile on the right where you will see a specially carved NDW seat. A grass path now takes you along a line of trees, and eventually by way of a stile onto a minor road (Grid ref: 858466). Turn left, and at a junction of lanes soon after bear left once more. Cross the River Wey, and then pass the entrance to the Campana International College and continue uphill along Compton Way. At the top of the slope where the lane curves to the right, go ahead on a fence-enclosed footpath, Wey Hanger. (Hanger refers to a woodland on a steep slope, and is often used in regard to the Downs.)

The path leads into a field where you follow the left-hand boundary to a woodland on the far side. Maintain direction through the woods, ignoring alternative paths until you descend to a crossing bridleway and turn right along a sandy trail. When this brings you to a fenced boundary bear left and, passing a large bungalow on the right, continue ahead alongside a drive which eventually leads to a road south of Runfold. Turn left. About 20 yards later turn right on another footpath among trees. This soon brings you to Sands Road (Grid ref: 873471) where you turn right. About a third of a mile along this road you come to Farnham Golf Clubhouse at a junction of lanes, and bear left into Blighton Lane.

After about 500 yards, when the lane curves left, take a footpath on the right which goes alongside a wooded garden. Remain on this path until it brings you to another country road, which you cross directly ahead into a region of arable farmland with wooded hills beyond.

On coming to a group of pine trees the path forks. Veer right, and at a fenced area bear right, then left, and keep alongside a hedge beyond which, hidden by a high bank, is a sand pit – the first of many extractions on the North Downs Way. Continue along the left-hand edge of two large open fields, and eventually come onto a country road opposite Landthorne Hatch Cottage, where you briefly turn right. (**Seale** is a short distance along the lane to the left.) In a few paces cross a stile on the left to gain a path alongside a wood. After about 250 yards cut off to the left, soon following a fence. When the fencing ends cross a stile and turn right, now walking along the top edge of a sloping meadow beside pinewoods (Payn's Firs) and with pleasant views ahead through a valley, flanked on the north side by the ridge of the Hog's Back.

At the end of the meadow go through a belt of woodland, gently sloping downhill. The path eventually swings right then left, and descends as a sunken pathway between steep banks on which foxgloves stand sentry-like in summer. The path spills onto a very narrow lane. Turn left, and in a few paces bear right opposite a red-brick bungalow. Cross a minor stream which (unseen) flows south into a series of ponds, and rise up a slope on an eroded, sandy path among trees to Puttenham Common. Towards the head of the slope honeysuckle and dog roses flank the path and, on warm summer days, fill the air with perfume.

Where the path forks on the crown of the hill, take the left-hand option through bracken, and at a crossing track by a noticeboard veer left. The way becomes a sunken path among more foxgloves, an undulating trail which brings you to the head of a drive by a house. Continue directly ahead on a track which feeds onto a narrow lane, and follow this down to **Puttenham** (*refreshments*), which you enter by the village Post Office Stores in The Street.

Puttenham is a trim village with some pleasant houses and cottages as you pass through. Keep ahead along The Street to reach *The Good*

Intent pub, and maintain direction towards the parish church of St John the Baptist. The road veers left around the church and comes to a T-junction by the gateway entrance to Puttenham Priory (Grid ref: 934479). Cross the B3000 with care, turn right and soon draw level with *The Jolly Farmer* (a Harvester pub/restaurant). Directly opposite this turn left on a gravel drive leading to a golf course.

After passing the clubhouse continue ahead. After a while pass a barn, then the way forks. Take the main left branch (the right-hand option goes to a cricket pavilion) and shortly after this it forks again. This time take the right branch, in effect straight ahead, along the edge of the golf course. After a while you pass houses, then the way narrows to enter woods. At a staggered crosstracks keep ahead; the track is now little more than footpath-wide and it takes you out to a metalled lane which goes beneath the A3 and a second road bridge adorned with two large wooden crosses.

Turn left at a T-junction, and in a few paces leave the road by the entrance to **Watts Gallery**.[3] (**Note:** *Refreshments are available at tearooms here.*) The North Downs Way journeys along a sandy track whose banks are honeycombed with rabbit warrens. After passing between barns the way narrows and rises uphill through woodland. At crosstracks continue ahead with the Loseley Estate's nature reserve on the right. Leaving trees behind the way cuts through deep sand, and coming to a junction of paths you veer left briefly on a track, then turn right on a stony track. Large aerial masts can be seen on the ridge to the left.

The track takes you beside more woods, becomes a metalled lane/farm drive, then a sandy track uphill. Through woods come to a T-junction of tracks and turn left. After about 30 yards the track, which has become a narrow surfaced lane, turns right and leads to Piccard's Farm, after which it reverts to a track once more. About ½ mile beyond the farm come onto a road and bear left. This leads to the A3100 opposite *Ye Olde Ship Inn*. Bear right, then take the next turning on the left, Ferry Lane. The lane slopes downhill, and over a railway bridge the slope is a steep one between houses. At the foot of the slope lies the River Wey on the southern outskirts of **Guildford**.[4]

Note: *For overnight accommodation and all facilities, turn left and follow the towpath for about ¾ mile to the centre of town.*

Bear right and cross a footbridge, and on the east bank of the river turn left for about 20 yards, then bear right when the path forks. Soon enter Shalford Park and cross straight ahead to the A281 (Grid ref: 999483) which you reach by a telephone kiosk and a bus stop. (Buses into Guildford.)

Items of Interest:

1: Farnham is overlooked by a 12th century castle built by Henri de Blois. Besieged by Cromwell, it belonged to the Bishops of Winchester until 1927, then the Bishop of Guildford held it until 1956. It is now a training centre, but the Norman keep is open to the public (☎ 01252 713393). North of the castle stretch the 300 acres of Farnham Park, while to the south, between the castle and the river, the town has some handsome Tudor and Georgian houses. In 1763 William Cobbet, politician, journalist and author of *Rural Rides*, was born here. The Romans settled in Farnham for something like 400 years, but the town's wealth came first through the cloth trade, then via brewing. At one time Farnham had no less than five breweries. The town has b&b and hotel accommodation, pubs, restaurants and an assortment of shops. (Tourist Information Centre: Vernon House, 28 West St, Farnham GU9 7DR ☎ 01252 715109.)

2: The River Wey is little more than a sluggish stream when first seen in Farnham, but is navigable from Weybridge to Godalming, passing through Guildford. In 1653 the River Wey Navigation gave access to the Thames and brought added prosperity to such places as Guildford. That navigation extended to Godalming in 1763, and stretched south for military purposes in 1816 as the Wey and Arun Canal, thus linking the Thames with the South Coast. However, with the coming of the railways the Canal became obsolete and closed in 1868. Where the North Downs Way crosses the river south of Guildford, the bankside footpath forms part of the Wey-South Path – 36 miles (58km) from Guildford to Amberley on the South Downs Way.

3: Watts Gallery is dedicated to the work of George Frederic Watts (1817–1904), the painter and sculptor who came to Compton with his second wife, Mary, who was also an artist. The gallery, designed by his friend Christopher Turnor and begun when Watts was 83, contains more than 200 of his works. Mary Watts was responsible for the extraordinary terracotta chapel situated a little further south, on the way to Compton.

4: Guildford is the county town of Surrey. It has a conspicuous red-brick 20th century cathedral which overlooks the nearby University of Surrey, and the keep of a Norman castle built on the east side of the river. In the High Street stands a group of 17th century almshouses and a very fine Guildhall with a famous clock overhanging the road, while the Angel Hotel boasts a wooden gallery and a coaching yard. In the Middle Ages Guildford prospered through the wool trade, but when that trade began to decline, it was replaced by the opening of the River Wey Navigation in the 17th century. Today the town is largely divided by the A3, and spills east and west into the surrounding countryside. But the heart of Guildford is graced by the River Wey which hints at a rural atmosphere. The town has all facilities, including b&b and hotel accommodation. (Tourist Information Centre: 14 Tunsgate, Guildford GU1 3QT ☎ 1483 444333.)

SECTION 2: GUILDFORD TO THE MOLE VALLEY (A24)

Distance:	**13 miles (21km)**
Maps:	**Harveys North Downs Way West 1:40,000**
	OS Landranger 186 Aldershot & Guildford and 187 Dorking, Reigate & Crawley 1:50,000
	OS Landranger 145 Guildford & Farnham and 146 Dorking, Box Hill & Reigate 1:25,000
Accommodation:	**Albury (+ 1 mile), Shere (+ 1 mile), Gomshall (+ 1 mile), Tanners Hatch Youth Hostel (+ ¾ mile), Ranmore Common, Dorking (+ 1 mile)**
Refreshments:	**Newlands Corner**

This stage is more strenuous than the previous one, for almost as soon as Guildford is left behind the North Downs Way makes the ascent of sandy St Martha's Hill, a splendid viewpoint at a height of 573ft (175m) from which, it is claimed, you can see six counties. The way crosses the hill and descends north before climbing onto the Downs proper and reaching another noted viewpoint at Newlands Corner. Thereafter the eastward trend resumes along the crest of the Downs, much of it through woodland, but emerging now and then to gain a wide panorama. At the end of the day the path slopes down to the Mole Valley above Dorking, passing a large vineyard and with Box Hill looming ahead as the next obstacle to be crossed at the beginning of the next stage of the walk.

From the A281 at Shalford Park cross with care and continue heading east along a residential street, The Pilgrims Way.[1] Rising gently the road curves slightly left, with a row of lime trees on the right-hand

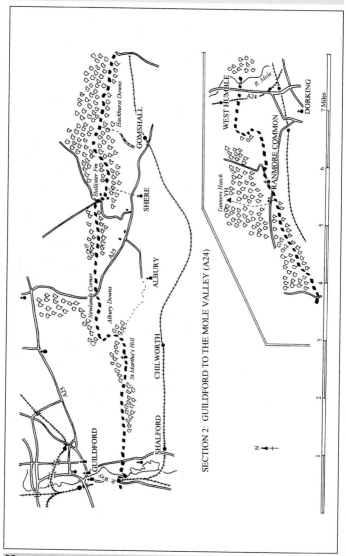

SECTION 2: GUILDFORD TO THE MOLE VALLEY (A24)

side. When these end veer right along a surfaced drive which soon ends in a small car park. Continue ahead, pass to the left of the white-painted Chantry Cottage, and enter Chantry Wood on a rough track. This mostly edges the wood, with NDW waymarks at path and track junctions. At the end of an open but fence-lined section, come to more woods, and at a crosstracks you maintain direction. The track has now narrowed to a bridleway, and when this becomes deeply cut, a footpath runs parallel with it on the right. Eventually join a stony path and continue ahead, still within the woods.

The path brings you to the narrow Halfpenny Lane where you bear left for a few paces, then turn right just beyond a 30mph sign to pass Southernway Cottage. Cross a drive and keep ahead on a sandy track which leads up to **St Martha's Hill**[2] (Grid ref: 027484). Pass along the left-hand side of the church which crowns the hill, and just beyond which you gain a magnificent panorama. Maintain direction on the east side of the church to descend a broad sandy track. Partway down the slope, and just before reaching a noticeboard announcing the start of the Downs Link, veer left on a more narrow path. This descends through woods, and immediately before it spills onto White Lane at the foot of the hill, you turn left, then right along a path which runs parallel with the lane.

Note: *If you intend to spend the night in **Albury**, turn right along the lane. This leads directly to the village.*

For some way the path keeps close company with the lane, but then it crosses and climbs through woods heading north-east. On leaving the woods the path forks. Take the left branch (in effect continuing ahead) to angle across **Albury Downs** with lovely views across the valley you've just crossed, to wooded hills beyond. Keep to the upper edge of the downland slope where seats have been placed to exploit the view, and from where it becomes evident that the North Downs Way has exchanged the sand hills for chalk. These are the real Downs at last.

The path slants up to **Newlands Corner** (*refreshments*) where there's a car park with public toilets and a refreshment kiosk. The North Downs Way proper just avoids the buildings by veering a little to the right, and crosses the A25 a few paces east of the car park entrance (Grid ref: 044493). Enter woods once more on a firm path by a NDW noticeboard, to follow an old Drove Road east for a little over 1½ miles (2½km), at which point you reach the West Hanger car park beside Staple Lane. Cross directly ahead, and after another stretch of woodland come onto Combe Lane by a concrete dew pond. Turn right, and in a few paces go left. The path soon brings you to a track where you veer slightly left. Keep to the track as it makes a sharp left-hand bend to **Hollister Farm**, after which you re-enter woodland. The way through the woods is on a partly surfaced track. At crosstracks note a large circular concrete tank on the right.

Note: *Should you plan to find accommodation in **Shere**, take the right-hand track and follow the bridleway through woods and down the slope, then cross the A25 with care to enter the village shortly after.*

Continue ahead and, almost a mile later, come to a second such tank – this one seen on the left at the Gravelhill Gate crosstracks. There's a seat here.

Note: *For accommodation in **Gomshall** turn right here. Down a steep slope come onto Colekitchen Lane which leads to Gomshall.*

The North Downs Way continues ahead for about a third of a mile where the way forks. Leave the main track and take the right branch. About 30 yards later come to a noticeboard giving information about **Hackhurst Downs**, and a sign directing the NDW to the right (Grid ref: 095491).

Sloping down a grass path, veer left on reaching a gate. Out of the woods cross a bare track and through a kissing gate continue on a grass path among trees and scrub. Go through a second kissing gate and bear right on a crossing path which leads to a third kissing gate giving access to the National Trust owned Blatchford Down which affords very fine views.

Leave Blatchford Down through yet another kissing gate, cross a rutted track (known as Beggars Lane) and maintain direction with more inspiring views to enjoy as you dodge in and out of woodland. In one of these woodland sections pass the first of several Second World War brick pillboxes followed by yet more fine views.

After passing through a gate on White Down Lees come to crossing paths and continue ahead, rising uphill to pass another pillbox on the right. Gaining height the way twists and turns, then comes to another path junction where a finger post sends you to the right on a sunken path to a road. Go down the road for a few paces, then cut left on a chalk path which soon takes you into woods again. Pass another pillbox, and yet another in a wooded area. On leaving the woods through a kissing gate you gain more lovely views, this time with the isolated church of Wotton seen down in the valley.

The way soon returns to woodland by a further pillbox, joins a track by yet another where you go through a gate and rise uphill. Near the head of the slope bear right when the track forks, and twist among trees along the edge of the steep scarp slope for some distance. At a crossing bridleway continue ahead following a line of beech trees. After a long stretch go through wooden bars to another crossing track and continue ahead with views of Dorking[3] ahead, and the wooded Leith Hill[4] with its tower visible to the south. After passing between another set of wooden bars, the way leads in an almost straight line through the woods.

A few paces before coming to the open meadow of Steer's Field at **Ranmore Common** (*accommodation*) – with the village church seen ahead – a path breaks off to the left. This is the one to take should you plan to stay overnight at Tanners Hatch Youth Hostel.

Note: *To reach **Tanners Hatch** bear left on the path which cuts through a final strip of woodland and brings you to Ranmore Common Road. Cross to the farthest left of three houses and take the track into woods on its left-hand side. Signs direct the way down to the youth hostel, which is reached about ¾ mile from the NDW on the edge of the Polesden Lacey estate (☎ 01306 877964).*

Go through the gate into Steer's Field and take the right-hand of two paths. On the far side of the meadow bear left and, through a gate, come to a road junction (Grid ref: 144504). Walk ahead along the road in the direction of Bookham and **West Humble**, passing the church of St Barnabas, then St Barnabas Old School next door. When the road makes a sharp left-hand bend, continue ahead briefly on a private drive by the entrance to Denbies. After about 20 yards turn right on a track lined with deer fencing. At crosstracks turn left and soon pass through tall gates above Denbies Vineyard.[5]

With vineyards spreading down the slope wander ahead along

the track, then go through another tall deer fence gate and you'll soon be overlooking the Mole Valley above which Box Hill rises on the far side. Continue ahead at crosstracks, and ignoring the first track on the right beyond these, the way forks a few paces after. Bear right. As you descend the slope so the track narrows. At the foot of the hill pass through a gate and walk ahead on a drive which leads beneath a Victorian railway bridge and out to the busy A24 (Grid ref: 170514).

Note: *Dorking* *lies 1 mile to the south. It has accommodation, refreshments and all services. Either turn right and walk alongside the road, or cross with care to a bus stop opposite.*

Items of interest:

1: The Pilgrims Way refers to the route commonly thought to have been taken by a penitent Henry II following the murder of Thomas à Becket in Canterbury Cathedral in 1170, and subsequently walked by countless pilgrims and recorded in Chauncer's *Canterbury Tales*. The route is 118 miles (190km) long, and it links Winchester with Canterbury. Today much of the Pilgrims Way is paved road, but there are long stretches of footpath and trackway too. (See *Guide to the Pilgrims Way and North Downs Way* by Christopher John Wright [Constable].) The name Pilgrims Way has in fact only fairly recently been adopted for this route.

2: St Martha's Hill to the east of Guildford stands at 573ft (175m), and is thought to have been a sacred site to Bronze Age settlers. The flint-walled church on the summit is said to be the only one in England with this dedication. Largely rebuilt in 1850, parts of the church date back to the 13th century, although the first Christian chapel to stand on the site was built there 200 years earlier. St Martha's is the parish church of Chilworth, a village lying at the southern foot of the hill.

3: Dorking stands astride Stane Street which the Romans built between Chichester and London – see Section 8 of *The South Downs Way* by Kev Reynolds (Cicerone). The Saxons settled here but discovery of Iron Age implements would suggest that they were not the first to choose the site. Beneath the town centre are several man-made caves and passages, the deepest being about 75ft (23m),

The trail heads through woodland towards Ranmore Common (Section 2)

Tanners Hatch, a youth hostel close to the North Downs Way (Section 2)

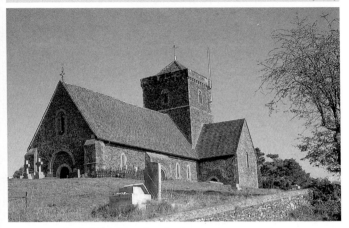

The lonely hilltop church of St Martha's, near Albury

rumoured to have been the haunt of smugglers. While the town's museum recalls its past, modern Dorking retains an attractive heart.

4: Leith Hill to the south-west of Dorking is, at 965ft (294m), the very crown of Surrey and the highest point in south-east England, from which (according to John Evelyn) '...may be discerned twelve or thirteen counties on a serene day'. On the summit stands a tower built in 1766 by Richard Hull, the eccentric squire of Leith Hill Place, who is buried there. The tower is 60ft (18m) high, and from the topmost platform the English Channel can sometimes be seen through the Shoreham Gap in the South Downs. In 1844 a group of surveyors stood on this platform and managed to identify no fewer than 41 of London's churches. Leith Hill is owned by the National Trust.

5: Denbies Vineyard is England's largest, an impressive fan of vines marching down the slope at the western outfall of the Mole Valley. The winery is open daily to the public.

SECTION 3: MOLE VALLEY (A24)
TO MERSTHAM

Distance:	**10 miles (16km)**
Maps:	**Harveys North Downs Way West 1:40,000**
	OS Landranger 187 Dorking, Reigate & Crawley 1:50,000
	OS Explorer 146 Dorking, Box Hill & Reigate 1:25,000
Accommodation:	**Box Hill, Betchworth (+ 1½ miles), Reigate (+ 1 mile), Redhill (+ 2 miles)**
Refreshments:	**Box Hill, Reigate Hill, Merstham**

Immediately after crossing the Mole Valley at the start of this stage, the North Downs Way climbs steeply to the top of Box Hill. It's a strenuous start to the day, but this is not the only climb, for the route makes a roller-coaster along the Downs before a final descent from Reigate Hill leads across less demanding terrain on the way to Merstham. Once again there are long woodland sections, but with sufficient openings to give broad views. Apart from Box Hill's much-heralded panorama, one of the very best is to be enjoyed from the open downland between Colley Hill and Reigate Hill.

The walk resumes on the east side of the A24 where a car park gives access to the River Mole[1] and the path to Box Hill. There are two ways of crossing the river. The most direct is by way of a series of stepping stones, but should the river be high, or you're uneasy, a footbridge offers an alternative crossing a little way to the north. Both options begin in the car park – for the stepping stones route take the path at the right-hand corner; for the footbridge leave the car park at its left-hand corner. The two routes come together a short distance beyond the river crossing.

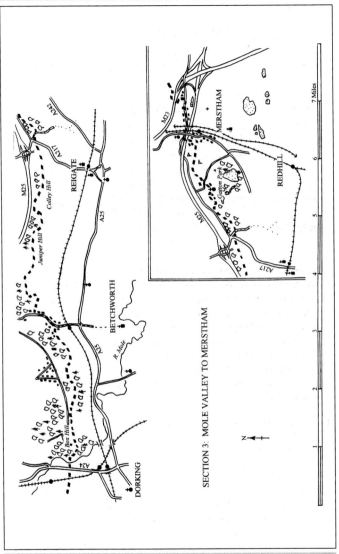

SECTION 3: MOLE VALLEY TO MERSTHAM

The way soon begins the steep climb to Box Hill, in places with the aid of steps cut in the hillside between trees and scrub. At the top of a long steep section go through a grove of yew trees, and at a crossing path bear right to gain a view onto Dorking. The path then curves and rises again over open downland to arrive at the trig point and viewing platform on **Box Hill**[2] (*accommodation, refreshments*). This is a noted beauty spot with magnificent views across the Weald. In the far distance a soft blue line hints at the South Downs.

Note: *For refreshments continue up the slope to a café and National Trust Visitor Centre. For accommodation, follow the narrow road east to* **Box Hill** *village.*

The North Downs Way continues beyond the trig point and on entering woodland the path forks. Bear left up the slope and just below a road you veer right to travel through the woods. Other paths break away, but the NDW is obvious. It crosses a couple of gully-like tracks, and having crossed the second of these the way angles slightly downhill. After a while it makes a sharp left-hand bend to climb once more by a series of steps to a broad track. Turn right, and when it cuts back sharply to the right as a hairpin, leave the track and go ahead to descend more steps. At the bottom of these turn left on a rising chalk path, still in woodland. The path carries on up the slope, near the head of which it forks. Take the right-hand option.

This narrow path contours across the wooded slope, but just before it starts to descend more wooden steps, note the stone memorial on the left dedicated to 'Quick – an English Thoroughbred'. Descend through what seems like a tunnel of trees, then out along an exposed bank with views again to Dorking. Care is required here after rain when the chalk can be very slippery. After descending for some way the path curves left to pass below a chalk quarry. It then makes a gentle traverse to the left among trees. Just before coming to a gate across the track, note the lime kiln to the right. Cross the track which links two sections of quarry, and continue ahead on a fenced path sloping downhill. This leads to the head of a narrow road lined with cottages. The road veers right to a T-junction where you turn left up Pebblehill Road (Grid ref: 210516).

Note: *For overnight accommodation in* **Betchworth** *turn right along Pebblehill Road (the B2032) for a little over a mile.*

There's a pavement on the left-hand side, and when this ends take a footpath up a slope among trees above the road. When this returns to the road cross with care and continue ahead. Pass three houses, then turn right on a footpath leading through a long avenue of mature trees and into a field where you bear left. A few paces later go through a bridle gate and maintain direction on the left-hand edge of a large field towards the foot of the wooded Downs. Go ahead up the slope, but when the path forks bear right. After contouring for a while the path then angles up the hillside and reaches a crossing track by a fence. Bear right.

The track returns the North Downs Way to the foot of the slope where you come to a path junction and bear left to climb steps. Soon cut off to the right and wander along the lower slopes for some way among trees and scrub and wild roses, gaining a profile of the North Downs plunging to low-lying farmland where the Weald stretches into the far distance. The path is eventually joined by another from the left near a fence. Veer slightly right ahead, then take the left-hand path when it forks. Through a strip of woodland and over a crossing path with steps on the left, continue ahead. For some way it continues a gently undulating course along the lower slope of **Juniper Hill**, but after crossing a bridleway you turn left to climb the Downs along a sunken track which eventually arrives at a narrow road by the entrance to Mole Place (Grid ref: 238523).

Bear right for about 20 yards, then turn right on a pathway among woods which leads onto the National Trust owned **Colley Hill**. Remain on the broad tarmac path to pass a brick water tower (if you stray to the right you'll be rewarded with big views), and a little under ½ mile later you come to a white, stone-pillared pavilion[3] with seats, erected in 1909. From here a far-reaching panorama makes the perfect excuse to rest for a few minutes.

Beyond the pavilion a track takes you past scars of the great storm of 1987, then an aerial mast and a large stone water tank on the left. The track becomes a lane, and when this turns sharp left, continue ahead on another track which slopes downhill and brings you to a footbridge over the A217. Come off the footbridge to a car park, with a National Trust refreshment kiosk and public toilets (Grid ref: 263524). Walk through the car park and cross a very narrow road, Wray Lane.

Note: *For accommodation in either **Reigate** or **Redhill**, turn right along Wray Lane which leads to both towns.*

Across the road enter **Gatton Park**[4] where a broad stony path slopes downhill. When it forks take the left branch and veer left at the next junction. Winding round the wooded hillside the track brings you close to a road and onto a drive by a white-painted house. Turn right along the drive and enter the grounds of Gatton Park School (the Royal Alexandra and Albert School). Wander through the grounds, keeping left of the buildings, and just past the chapel turn left at a junction of drives to leave the school grounds by a neat thatched gatehouse, North Lodge (Grid ref: 276532).

Continue ahead on the road, but bear left after 100 yards on a tarmac drive, and when this curves left go ahead along a track. A footpath continues between hedges through a section of golf course with the M25 ahead. The NDW is waymarked across the golf course, crossing a narrow lane and ahead beside a windbreak of trees, then over a more open section, beyond which a path leads alongside Merstham cricket ground – the Club was founded in 1864. So come into **Merstham** (*refreshments*) at Quality Street (Grid ref: 289534). *The Feathers* pub and shops will be found a short distance to the right.

Merstham rests at the foot of the Downs on a narrow belt of Upper Greensand and, like neighbouring Reigate, Gatton, Bletchingley and Godstone, was once noted for its sandstone quarries. Merstham's quarry provided stone for the building of Windsor Castle. (The same stone is found near Farnham, where it is known as Malmstone.) The houses which line Quality Street hint of more gentle times than today's, for poor Merstham now suffers the indignity of having two railways and two of Britain's busiest motorways passing nearby. There are pubs and shops, railway to Croydon, London, Redhill and Gatwick, and bus services to Redhill.

Items of Interest:

1: The River Mole has cut a trench through the North Downs which allowed the Romans to carry their Chichester to London road (Stane Street) close to Box Hill, over which the otherwise straight alignment would have taken it. Milton, Pope and Spenser all alluded to the river's supposed tendency to burrow (as the name might suggest), but their poetic musings have little place in geological fact. Milton's '...sullen Mole that runneth underneath' merely runs under widespread branches of riverbank trees – not the chalk of the hefty Downs. Just north of the stepping stones by which the NDW crosses the river stands the *Burford Bridge Hotel*, formerly known as the *Fox and Hounds*, where Nelson and Lady Hamilton said farewell before Nelson sailed for Trafalgar. George Meredith (1828–1909), poet and novelist, lived nearby in Flint Cottage.

2: Box Hill also has a place in literature, for in *Emma*, Jane Austen placed a picnic party there. As a popular beauty spot it is well known, and the 17th century diarist John Evelyn wrote in praise of the yews and box trees for which it is named: '...it seeming from these evergreens to be summer all the winter.' Many of the box trees, however, were cut down in the 18th century for use as engraving blocks. Now owned by the National Trust, Box Hill was created a Country Park in 1971. From the 563ft (172m) summit of the hill a huge panorama spreads across the Weald, and includes part of the Greensand Ridge and distant South Downs.

3: The Stone Pavilion on Reigate Hill was erected in 1909 by Lieutenant-Colonel Robert William Inglis, and presented to the Borough of Reigate for the benefit of local people. It has a blue ceiling adorned with gold stars, an orientation table surrounded by seats, and commanding views.

4: Gatton Park was a one-time 'rotten borough' that, until 1832, returned two full Members of Parliament, even though there were no more than 23 houses in the village. The Park is part of an extensive estate whose house (built 1830) was destroyed by fire in 1934. St Andrew's Church dates from the 15th century, and stands near the present Royal Alexandra and Albert School.

SECTION 4: MERSTHAM TO
WESTERHAM HILL

Distance:	12¼ miles (20km)
Maps:	Harveys North Downs Way West 1:40,000
	OS Landranger 187 Dorking, Reigate & Crawley and 188 Maidstone & The Weald of Kent 1:50,000
	OS Explorer 146 Dorking, Box Hill & Reigate and 147 Sevenoaks & Tonbridge 1:25,000
Accommodation:	Oxted (+ 1 mile)
Refreshments:	The Harrow pub, south of Caterham, and another on Botley Hill

Happily the route soon leaves motorways behind and resumes along the crest of the Downs among arable fields and woodlands, skirting south of Caterham and, east of the A22, passing above another vineyard. After wandering through a woodland section on Oxted Downs, the path suddenly descends a long and very steep stairway created directly above the tunnel which carries the Oxted to London Victoria railway through the North Downs, and presents a remarkable bird's-eye view directly onto it as it emerges from the tunnel. East of this the way crosses the line of the Greenwich Meridian and at last leaves Surrey to enter Kent above Westerham.

Turn left in Merstham's Quality Street and near the end – just past The Old Forge, a handsome Tudor house – take a footpath on the right which crosses the M25 on a footbridge and shortly brings you to a road opposite St Katherine's Church. Turn right, and at the A23 dual carriageway cross with care, then walk ahead along Rockshaw Road. This crosses two railway lines. Keep along the road for another ½ mile, and at the end of an open meadow section, turn left on a

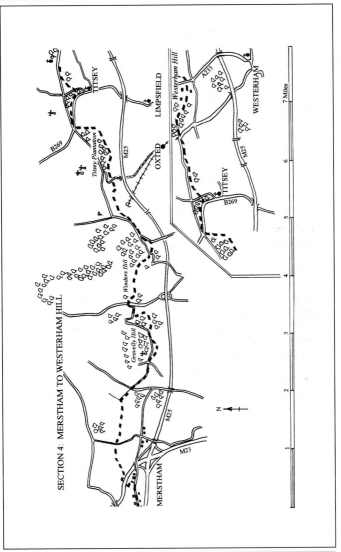

SECTION 4: MERSTHAM TO WESTERHAM HILL

footpath by a bungalow. This descends through a flowery meadow and goes beneath the M23. On the other side follow a track as it swings round to the right and up into a meadow. A bridleway then slants up the hillside, goes through scrub tangled with wild clematis, and out to a large field where the way angles half-right uphill. On reaching the head of the slope bear right on what becomes a hedge-lined track. This leads to a country road where you cross ahead on a gravel drive, passing a large red tile-hung house, and continue past several more houses that enjoy wide views. The drive ends near a house called Hilltop whose front is adorned by a clock. Continue ahead, now on a track, and ignoring other footpaths and bridleways breaking from it, come to a lane by Willey Park Farm. Just beyond this come to a junction of minor lanes and bear right (Grid ref: 323543).

An elderly man with a fluff of white hair and grey cardigan was studying the signpost, squinting against the light while his wife sat patiently in the car nearby. 'Are you lost?' I asked. 'No, no. Just wondered what it said.' He looked me up and down. 'Having a little walk then?' he asked. 'Yes, it's a lovely day for a stroll.' 'How far are you going?' 'Dover,' I said. 'Dover? Walking to Dover? Bloody worsteds!' 'Not today, I'm following the North Downs Way.' 'What's that?' I told him. 'Bloody worsteds,' he exclaimed again. 'Dover!' Then: 'Very interesting town, Dover. Very historic. Stationed there in the war, you know. Up on the castle, watching the Battle of Britain overhead. Gunfire, shells, the lot. Hitler's doodlebugs; everything. Evelyn Laye was entertaining the troops. She and her husband. Afterwards stayed for a troop dance. We all queued up to get a dance with her, you know.' He continued to unravel his war experiences – the Near East, then the Far East – and I was beginning to think I'd be there until sunset, when suddenly he said, 'Still, you'll be wanting to get on – if you're walking to Dover.' We shook hands and I turned away. As I did I heard him say to his wife, 'D'you hear that? He's walking to Dover!' Then came his wife's voice, pinched, high and strangely delicate in view of her words: 'Dover? Bloody worsteds!'

On coming to Stanstead Road note that *The Harrow* pub (*refreshments*) is found a short distance to the left. Cross ahead into

War Coppice Road, a tree-lined lane which is followed for almost ¾ mile (wild garlic beside the road in springtime). At a minor crossroads, mount a stile at the entrance to Hextalls Lane and continue parallel with War Coppice Road, through woodland. The way gradually loses height, goes between wooden bars and veers left to a crossing track. Continue ahead and at another broad crossing track bear left and follow this uphill to a grassy viewing area on **Gravelly Hill** (Grid ref: 341534).

Bear right along the road, and at the end of the grass area turn right again on a stony track which leads down the slope among woods of beech and ash. At crosstracks maintain direction, but at the next fork take the right-hand option. The path cuts round the hillside with the slope dropping away quite steeply. Descend steps and continue through woods, curving among mature trees, and down a second flight of steps. The path continues to a narrow road, but immediately before reaching this break off to the right and cross a footbridge over the A22. Over a stile on the east side of the bridge cross a narrow meadow to a second stile by a field gate. There you turn right along a track, but after about 100 yards bear left on a footpath curving through more woods, then down steps onto a lane near a warehouse. Cross to the continuing path – a very untidy patch – then up more steps onto a concrete drive where you turn right.

Passing **Winders Hill** Cottage a track continues above a vineyard and comes to a narrow road by a small lodge. Bear right, then left onto a footpath which leads uphill in the direction of Marden Park and Great Church Woods – neither of which are visited by the North Downs Way. However, the path takes you into woodland where it eventually forks by a large beech tree. Take the right-hand option and after a while leave the woods at a narrow country road. Cross to a continuing fence-lined path sloping downhill. At the foot of the slope cross a stile on the left and follow a path which keeps above Tandridgehill Lane for a while before bringing you onto the lane itself. Bear left, and in a few paces turn right at a T-junction. After about 120 yards along this road a footpath runs parallel with it on the right. At a T-junction of paths turn right, and down the slope a few paces bear left at the next finger post along an undulating path among trees. At a crossing path descend a long and very steep flight of steps built directly above the Oxted railway tunnel (Grid ref: 375541).

At the bottom of the steps there is an amazing view along the railway line to Oxted and the Greensand Ridge beyond. Turn left through trees, then out across the open slopes of Oxted Downs before descending and going round the fenced boundary of a chalk quarry. The path eventually comes onto a narrow road by a house (Grid ref: 385543). Turn right for about 20 yards, then left through a gap in a hedge.

Note: *Walkers seeking accommodation in* **Oxted** *should continue down this road for about 1 mile. Oxted has shops, restaurants and trains to Croydon and London Victoria.*

The continuing path ascends a few steps, then steeply up the slope, but when it forks you bear right on a gentle traverse path alongside a fence. When this ends turn downhill, sharing for a moment the route of the Vanguard Way,[1] then left along the top edge of a large field. Passing alongside **Titsey Plantation** you cross the (unmarked) line of the Greenwich Meridian. Eventually descend a few steps onto a sunken track known as Pitchfork Lane. Bear left and wander up the wooded slope until the track spills out at a road junction on Botley Hill.

Note: *For refreshments continue a short distance to the left along the B269 where there is a pub, the* Botley Hill Farmhouse.

Turn right briefly on the B269, then cross to a triangle of grass where the North Downs Way enters woods and keeps just above the road as it descends to Limpsfield. The path goes down the slope for some way, then cuts left to ascend a steep flight of steps, at the top of which you continue uphill, now alongside the woods. Over a stile the path continues slightly right ahead, and skirts the edge of more woodland with views to the right over the Holmesdale Valley – the valley that lies between the North Downs and Greensand Ridge and stretches as far east as Sevenoaks.

On reaching a very narrow lane turn right for a few paces, then left on a path entering woods again. Sloping gently downhill you emerge at the far side into a field, then cross slightly left towards a woodland crown. On the lower corner of this woodland cross a stile and walk alongside the woods. Following these you come close to a road opposite Clark's Lane Farm. Do not go onto the road but bear right along the top edge of the field, and at the far boundary cross a

A diversion from the way leads to Westerham, gateway into Kent

stile and continue beside a fence, then a hedge – but look for another stile on the left which takes the path up the slope via steps and out to a junction of roads (Grid ref: 416560).

Cross over to Church Hill, then bear right along Chestnut Avenue which you follow for a little over ½ mile. When it reaches a T-junction bear right. Passing a few houses you come to the Surrey/Kent boundary, marked by a NDW milestone indicating you've walked 48 miles from Farnham, but have 65 miles still to walk to Canterbury, or 77 to Dover. Now in Kent the metalled lane becomes a gravel drive which later deteriorates, and after another ½ mile or so, brings you to the A233 on the slopes of **Westerham Hill** (Grid ref: 441559).

Note: *For refreshments in **Westerham** turn right and wander beside the road for about 1½ miles. Westerham is an attractive and historic small town with shops and a good selection of cafés and restaurants, and a rather expensive hotel. Also bus link with Biggin Hill and Bromley which passes the NDW crossing of the A233. (Tourist Information Centre: Motorway Services Area, Clackett Lane, Westerham TN16 2ER ☎ 01959 565063.)*

Items of Interest:

1: The Vanguard Way is a 62 mile (100km) recreational walk which begins at East Croydon railway station and heads south to cross the North Downs, then continues over the Greensand Ridge, the Weald, Ashdown Forest and South Downs. The original finish was on Seaford Head, but it has since been lengthened as far as Newhaven. (See *The Wealdway & The Vanguard Way* by Kev Reynolds [Cicerone], and *The Vanguard Way* by the Vanguard Rambling Club.)

SECTION 5: WESTERHAM HILL
TO WROTHAM

Distance:	13¾ miles (22km)
Maps:	Harveys North Downs Way West 1:40,000
	OS Landranger 188 Maidstone & The Weald of Kent 1:50,000
	OS Explorer 147 Sevenoaks & Tonbridge 1:25,000
Accommodation:	Knockholt, Chevening (+ ½ mile), Dunton Green, Otford, Kemsing Youth Hostel (+ ½ mile), Wrotham
Refreshments:	Knockholt, Knockholt Pound, Dunton Green, Otford, Wrotham

This is a walk of three parts. Between Westerham Hill and Turvin's Farm east of Chevening much of the route is among arable farmland, and with the scarp slope hidden by trees one forms little indication that the path is actually journeying along the Downs – although when it does come to true downland the short-cropped turf is springy and rich in wild flowers. Then with the crossing of that open basin of land where the little River Darent makes its break through the Downs north of Sevenoaks, the North Downs Way is forced to tread tarmac around Dunton Green, and after a brief oasis of field and meadow, returns to tarmac again for the walk through Otford. But after climbing out of Otford and a short spell among woods, the downland nature of the walk is restored, and broad panoramas once more reward the miles.

Note: *Should the distance between Westerham and Wrotham be a little farther than you'd prefer for a single section of the walk, either Otford or Kemsing would make a convenient alternative end to this stage.*

From the A233 above Westerham cross with care to a stile on the east side which gives access to a large open field where you turn left and walk up the headland. Note that the oak finger posts on the North Downs Way in Surrey have now given way to the green metal posts of Kent. On gaining the top corner of the field maintain direction among trees and scrub, eventually emerging in the top corner of a second large field. Again turn left and follow the boundary with long views across the Holmesdale Valley. Before reaching the end of the field the way curves up some steps among trees. Over a stile continue up a grass slope to another stile, and maintain direction through woodland. On meeting a track bear right, and this will bring you to a steeply sloping meadow high above Pilgrim House. The way takes you across the head of the slope to a stile right of a field gate, and onto a track. Follow the left-hand boundary of the next field, at the top of which you find yourself on the very crest of the Downs (Grid ref: 449567).

Remain within the field and head to the right along the top boundary. In the far corner a double stile takes you into a narrow meadow where you wander ahead, but halfway along the boundary look for a stile on the left – this is almost hidden in the hedge. Over this turn right on a hedge-lined path. When it forks bear left and cross yet another stile, then along the continuing path through a patch of sparse woodland. The way curves round a hollow and along a line of mature trees.

On coming to a stile on the woodland edge do not cross, but turn sharply to the right and follow the line of a fence across a meadow. On the far side bear left over another stile and walk along the edge of a series of adjoining fields parallel with a country lane, until you emerge to a junction of narrow roads (Grid ref: 458574). Cross directly ahead to enter another field and maintain direction. Brasted Hill Farm can be seen off to the right. On the far side cross another narrow road and continue on the left-hand edge of a small field. The next field is much larger, is divided by wire fences with stiles linking each section, and with Brasted Lane the other side of the left-hand hedge. When you draw level with a white house another stile takes you into a large field bordering Roughfield Woods, with two tall radio masts seen slightly left ahead. Walk alongside the woods and maintain direction in the next adjoining field, but on entering a third

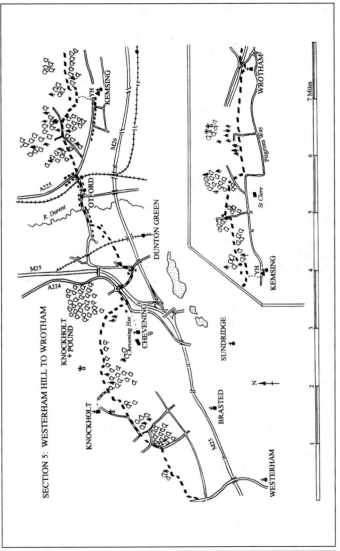

SECTION 5: WESTERHAM HILL TO WROTHAM

WROTHAM

KEMSING

YH

M26

OTFORD

A225

R. Darent

DUNTON GREEN

M25

A224

KNOCKHOLT + POUND

Chevening Hse

CHEVENING

SUNDRIDGE

KNOCKHOLT

St Clere

Pilgrims Way

KEMSING

YH

N

BRASTED

M25

WESTERHAM

1 2 3 4 5 6 7 Miles

field through a gap in the hedge, bear left along the headland. Near the top of this the way veers slightly left, then right along a track which goes along the right-hand edge of a narrow field. When the track curves right to spill onto a lane, remain within the field but turn left for about 80 yards, then down steps to cross the road (Grid ref: 471587).

Note: *Should you be seeking accommodation or refreshment in* **Knockholt***, turn left and left again at a T-junction.*

On the east side of the road keep to the right-hand edge of a field alongside an extensive woodland whose boundaries will be followed for the next mile or so. The path is clearly waymarked, and after passing through a largely open section of woodland, it cuts south, then north-east again with the woods still on your right-hand side. In the latter stages of this woodland boundary walk views are of Knockholt Pound to the left, and tall buildings of London seen in the distance – a reminder that for a while the North Downs Way sneaks just beyond the capital's outer limits. There is no real sense of downland here, though no suggestion of height either as the North Downs rise gently from the Thames, and it is only when the scarp edge is rediscovered that the true nature of the Downs as a barrier above the Weald becomes apparent. At last come onto another very narrow road by a bungalow and turn right (Grid ref: 485592).

Note: *There's a further opportunity for refreshment here by turning left along the road for less than ½ mile. Knockholt Pound has two pubs.*

A few paces after coming onto the road bear left through a kissing gate and wander ahead towards Lees Wood. Off to the right a view shows beyond the hinted Holmesdale Valley to the wooded Greensand Ridge. When you reach Lees Wood veer slightly left and follow a track round to the right through a gap, and on emerging cross a stile and bear right along the woodland edge. Towards the southern end the field narrows, and the path swings left into the woods, then bears left out of the trees to gain a view down the slope to stately **Chevening House**,[1] Chevening Church to the left of that and the large white building of Coombe Bank (now a private girls' school) above and to the right of Chevening House.

The North Downs Way takes you over a stile, then left round the edge of a steep downland slope. Views are splendid – across a great basin formed by a confluence of valleys walled by the greensand hills to the south. Keeping woods to your left the way soon contours south-east with Chipstead Lakes[2] seen down in the basin. Were it not for the M25, M26 and A21 complex below, this would be an idyllic and very peaceful corner. The way crosses a stile, still beside woods, and continues along the top edge of a large arable field to pass a seat which marks the 10th anniversary (in 1997) of Sevenoaks Ramblers. The path now goes down the slope with dog roses and elder flowers garlanding the descent in early summer. Near the foot of the slope go over a stile and down some steps into a field across which you can see Turvin's Farm. Go round the left-hand boundary and out to a road at the far corner (Grid ref: 496579).

Note: *If you have arranged accommodation in **Chevening**, turn right here, and shortly after passing Turvin's Farm take a path which strikes directly across the fields to Chevening Church.*

Donnington Manor Hotel marks the point at which the North Downs Way leaves Dunton Green

Turn left on the B2211 which parallels the M25, and after about 200 yards you'll find a pavement on the right-hand side. On coming to a roundabout turn right to cross the motorway. Now walk alongside the A224 towards **Dunton Green** (*accommodation, refreshments*). Reaching a junction by the *Rose & Crown* pub, turn left – this is also the route of the Darent Valley Path.[3] Immediately before reaching *Donnington Manor Hotel* (Grid ref: 506581) turn right on a footpath which leads into a field. Maintain direction along the right-hand edge, cross a stile and continue up a sloping field. At the head of the slope the path leads through a strip of woodland and emerges to a view across Otford rooftops to the North Downs on the far side of the Darent Valley.

The way cuts directly through the field ahead with views left into the Darent Valley.[4] Cross a railway bridge to the head of narrow Telston Lane and follow this down past New Barn Farm, then through a residental area to a T-junction where you turn right. This leads to the heart of **Otford** (*accommodation, refreshments*),[5] crossing on the way the innocent-looking River Darent.

Otford has four pubs, a restaurant, café and shops – all on the route of the North Downs Way. There's also a public toilet (on the left, opposite The Bull*), buses to Sevenoaks, and railway station serving London. (Tourist Information Centre: Buckhurst Lane, Sevenoaks TN13 1LQ ☎ 01732 450305.)*

Passing the village duckpond on your right walk ahead up Station Road (the A225), and turn into the first turning on the right after Otford Station. This is Pilgrims Way East. After about 100 yards take a path on the left rising up a few steps, then continue between hedges and fences to climb Otford Mount. A memorial seat makes the most of a view over Otford, and here the path veers slightly right and continues to climb more steps. Easing through woodland you then cross a hilltop field along its right-hand boundary and come to a junction of minor roads (Grid ref: 544599).

Walk ahead (direction Woodlands, East Hill and West Kingsdown), and after about 150 yards find a footpath on the right which is guided by a fence along the edge of Rowdow Wood. At the woodland corner the path is led by more stiles and a series of kissing gates through linking fields to reach another narrow lane by a house. Turn right, and shortly after veer left on a private drive leading to Otford Manor (formerly Hildenborough Hall). Just before the drive passes between brick pillars cross a stile on the right and follow a fence-lined path alongside woods. The way goes downhill among trees, comes to a crossing path, and continues down a few more paces to a bench seat on Whiteleaf Down (Grid ref: 552595).

Note: *If you plan to stay overnight at* **Kemsing Youth Hostel** *continue down the slope into Kemsing village and bear left. The hostel is located behind the church (☎ 01732 761341).*

The North Downs Way turns left to contour the hillside through patches of scrub above **Kemsing**,[6] and when the path forks at the start of a brief open stretch of downland, take the left branch uphill a little. Cross a deeply-sunken track in woods (the way down also goes to Kemsing YH) and continue ahead, soon crossing a stile and climbing a few steps, then through a group of oak trees to regain the crest of the Downs. A splendid panorama is won from this high point – one of the best of the walk so far. Note the wooden cross on the lip of the escarpment. Maintain direction across the downland turf, near the end of which you bear left over a stile and walk round the right-hand edge of a field. About 30 yards left of the right-hand corner cross another stile onto a continuing path which cuts along the edge of Fab's Wood.

Over a crossing track turn right onto a path which runs parallel with it, going through the wood and into an open field. Maintain direction to a stile on the far side which grants access to another woodland path, then into a second meadow. Continue ahead, passing above a house with a tennis court. About three-quarters of the way along this meadow turn right, then through a kissing gate to go left downhill among trees and onto Cotman's Ash Lane (Grid ref: 567598).

Walk uphill for a short distance. Just after passing the entrance to Summeryards, turn right by a barn and go straight ahead on a farm track into a meadow with another barn where you maintain direction – with the radio mast on Wrotham Hill now in view. Continue through the next meadow, but in the top left-hand corner a stile on the left leads the way as a woodland path. Twisting through Summeryards Wood you then emerge in the corner of a hilltop field

Wrotham marks the midway point between Farnham and Dover

and maintain direction along the broad headland. Veer right at a crossing track. This takes you round the head of another field, soon passing a NDW milestone – Farnham 60; Canterbury 54; Dover 65 miles.

Shortly after this the farm track curves right, but you veer left into the edge of a little woodland to pass a concrete dewpond, then walk ahead along the right-hand boundary of a large field. At the end of this enter Birches Wood where bluebells are abundant in springtime. This woodland, and much of the farmland around it, belongs to the **St Clere** Estate,[7] based at the foot of the Downs. Emerging from the woods on a country road turn right, but after about 20 yards take the footpath on the left. Descend steps to gain a lovely view across the Weald, with the line of the eastern Downs on the far side of the Medway Valley. Descend the slope to another stile, over which you walk ahead through an arable field as far as a narrow lane – **Pilgrims Way** (Grid ref: 583595).

Turn left along a hedge-lined track for about ¾ mile where you come to a narrow country road. Turn right, then in a couple of paces go left on a path which leads to **Wrotham** (*accommodation, refreshments*). Enter Wrotham along a residential street, and at crossroads continue ahead on the Pilgrims Way. After passing some houses the road bends to the right towards playing fields. On reaching tennis courts the North Downs Way cuts left on a tarmac path.

Wrotham has three pubs, a hotel (The Bull), b&b, shops, public toilets (about 200 yards past the tennis courts), telephone kiosk, and bus services to Borough Green (railway), Sevenoaks and Gravesend. The large medieval church, dedicated to St George, has a fine collection of brasses, and behind it there once stood a palace used by the peripatetic Archbishops of Canterbury. It was pulled down in 1349, and the stone used to build Archbishop Islip's palace in Maidstone. Wrotham was a staging post on the London road, and it was here in 1536 that Henry VIII learned that Anne Boleyn's execution had been carried out.

Items of Interest:

1: Chevening House was bequeathed to the nation on the death of the seventh Earl Stanhope in 1967 (together with a £250,000 endowment for its upkeep), and is now the official country home of the Foreign Secretary. A 17th century manor designed by Inigo Jones, it was in the Stanhope family from 1718 on.

2: Chipstead Lakes have been formed by flooding one-time gravel pits, and are now used as a wildfowl reserve.

3: The Darent Valley Path follows the modest River Darent from Sevenoaks to Dartford, passing several places of interest along the way, including Lullingstone Roman Villa. Kent County Council has published an illustrated guide to the walk.

4: The Darent Valley is one of the best-loved in this part of Kent, and with two pleasant villages (Shoreham and Eynsford) between Otford at its southern end, and Farningham where the valley's character changes. Artist Samuel Palmer lived for seven years in Shoreham beside the River Darent. Further downstream the Romans had a villa at Lullingstone near Eynsford, while the remains of Eynsford Castle (also beside the

Darent) date from Norman times. When the M25 was originally planned it was proposed to route it through the valley. Had the series of well-orchestrated protests by local people been unsuccessful it would have lost its peace and beauty for all time. Happily the motorway was rerouted to pass above and to the west of the valley.

5: Otford is an attractive village with a 2000 year history. The Romans were here, and Offa, King of Mercia, fought an important battle nearby in AD774, while another battle, this one against the Danes, took place in 1016. Near the church stand the ruins of one of the Archbishop's palaces, used by Becket, enlarged by Warham in the 16th century, but taken by Henry VIII from Archbishop Cranmer. Henry, however, preferred to stay at Knole in Sevenoaks and having barely used Otford Palace it quickly fell into disrepair. The church of St Bartholomew is worth a visit, while the duckpond in the centre of the village roundabout is said to be the only area of water in England designated as a listed building.

6: Kemsing has grown with commuter sprawl, but the old part of the village retains its character and repays a visit. The church of St Mary the Virgin is of Norman origin, while behind a village war memorial lies St Edith's Well in a little sunken garden. This is named for the daughter of King Edgar who was born here in AD961, and water from the spring is said to cure sore eyes.

7: St Clere Estate has at its heart a mansion built in the reign of Charles I for Sir John Sedley, known at the time as 'the hottest Parliamentarian in the county'. The house sits at the foot of the North Downs midway between Kemsing and Wrotham, but the estate land extends to the crest of the Downs and beyond.

SECTION 6: WROTHAM TO THE MEDWAY

Distance:	10½ miles (16½km)
Maps:	Harveys North Downs Way West 1:40,000
	OS Landranger 188 Maidstone & The
	Weald of Kent and 178 The Thames
	Estuary 1:50,000
	OS Explorer 147 Sevenoaks & Tonbridge
	and 148 Maidstone & The Medway Towns
	1:25,000
Accommodation:	Trottiscliffe (+ ¾ mile), Ryarsh (+ 1 mile),
	Birling (+ 1 mile), Rochester (+ 1¾ miles)
Refreshments:	Vigo, Trosley Country Park, Cuxton

The majority of this stage of the walk travels along the back of the Downs in a region of large fields and woodlands, and with long stretches devoid of habitation. This is the more surprising when you study a large-scale map of the area and note just how busy it seems with motorways and towns. But it is only by following footpaths that you can properly understand the truth of any landscape – such is the reality between Wrotham and Rochester along the North Downs Way. When long views are won, they often show scenes of distant industry, but now and then a secretive fold of downland is revealed, although most views are crowded by dense woodland.

Out of Wrotham the tarmac path east of the tennis courts leads onto the A20 where you turn left, crossing the M20. Immediately over the bridge turn right into the Pilgrims Way where, after about 100 yards or so, you will find a parallel path on the right-hand side. This returns you to the road by the entrance to Chaucers. You then continue downhill until reaching the entrance to another house on the left, then cross a stile into a field and walk along its right-hand boundary.

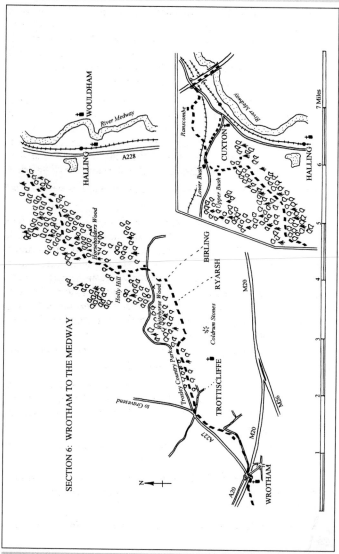

SECTION 6: WROTHAM TO THE MEDWAY

At the end of this field a pair of stiles directs the path into the next field ahead. Maintain direction, but on reaching yet another stile descend some steps onto the road once more and continue ahead. After passing a couple of houses take the second footpath on the left when the road begins to rise uphill. Once again follow the right-hand boundary of the field, and in the corner enter Hognore Wood.

Come onto a track and maintain direction towards a field gate. Take the left branch when the track forks and steadily rise up the wooded slopes of Trottiscliffe Down. Eventually arrive at the A227, walk up the road a short distance to *The Vigo Inn*, then turn right on a minor road. Just before this passes beneath a flint-built arch veer left up steps to enter **Trosley Country Park**[1] at a junction of tracks.

Note: *For accommodation in* **Trottiscliffe** *continue down the road for another ¾ mile.*

Should you need refreshments take the left branch and in a few paces come to a car park and Visitor Centre with refreshment kiosk (Grid ref: 633610). The North Downs Way follows the right branch ahead through the Country Park, now on a broad, firm track among woods on a fairly level course for a little over a mile, at which point it curves leftwards, rising to a barrier and a kissing gate leading out of the Park. Turn right on another track to descend the wooded slope, at the foot of which you come to the head of the metalled Pilgrims Way and the route of the Wealdway.[2]

Note: *A short stroll to the south lie the Coldrum Stones, remnants of a Neolithic Long Barrow beside the Wealdway.*

Turn left onto a narrow path which hugs the lower slopes of the Downs among trees and scrub for ¾ mile, ignoring other path options. Pass a square brick building on the left, and about 250 yards later the path curves right and forks.

Note: *For accommodation in* **Ryarsh** *take the right-hand option to Park Farm, then follow the lane beyond that.*

For the continuing North Downs Way take the left-hand path for another ¼ mile where views open across large flat fields. Shortly after come to a crossing path.

Note: *If you have arranged accommodation in* **Birling** *turn right here.*

At the crossing path turn left through a wide gap in the hedge, then over a stile and straight ahead between fences to the foot of the Downs. Here the way cuts to the right and makes a steep climb among scrub to emerge at the noted viewpoint of **Holly Hill** (Grid ref: 671624).

Emerging onto a road opposite Holly Hill Lodge walk ahead on a narrow lane. After the strenuous climb up the downland slope the lane gives a welcome opportunity to regain your composure. Keep on the lane beyond Holly Hill car park, and continue ahead when the tarmac ends by West Wing Holly Hill House. A stony track enters woods and forks. Take the right branch, and at the next fork continue on the left branch. The way is mostly firm underfoot and fairly level, but on sloping gently downhill you come to a crossing track. (This is about ½ mile or so after entering the woods.) Bear right then left into the corner of a field, across which two lines of power cables are carried by pylons (Grid ref: 673643).

The path leads directly ahead through the field, passing beneath one set of cables. On the far side, virtually beneath the second cable line, come to a track leading to the right-hand field. Cross the track through a gap in the hedge, and over a second track onto a footpath which cuts through a narrow belt of woodland to another field surrounded on all sides by trees. Again, cross directly ahead. Over a track on the far side the footpath maintains direction through a kissing gate into Ten Acre Wood.

Out of these woods come to a large open field with a marker post in the middle, seen slightly right ahead. Cross to Pastead Wood on the far side and continue. Eventually the path curves to the right along the woodland edge and comes to a 5-way junction of paths and tracks (Grid ref 689648).

I perched on a log to chew an apple, listening to the lazy croak and caw of rooks that circled over a neighbouring woodland. Then a lone walker emerged on one of the tracks, panting heavily and with sweat glistening on his face. Seeing me there he looked distinctly relieved. 'You wouldn't know the way to Luddesdown, would you?' he asked. I opened the map, pointed out where we were and indicated the path to take. 'Thanks,' he gasped. 'I've walked it several times before, but always with a friend who knows the way. This time I must have taken the wrong path … didn't know where the devil I was. Got in a bit of a panic, must admit.' Watching him go, I recalled something I read long ago: No-one goes so far nor so fast as the man who does not know where he's going.

The North Downs Way veers right ahead – in effect this is the second track on the right. It winds through the woods and passes beneath more power lines. In Wingate Wood the way is led along a narrow tree-lined spur, with the escarpment falling unseen towards North Halling to the right, and into an inner downland valley (also unseen) to the left. At a junction of paths below another power line, turn left and descend a steep flight of steps into a field. The path strikes ahead through the field to a kissing gate by a quarry entrance, then up the slope ahead alongside a fence. Off to the right the oasthouses of Dean Farm, minus their distinctive white cowls, can be clearly seen.

The Coldrum Stones, remains of a Neolithic burial chamber at the foot of the Downs

Now walk ahead through North Wood and out to a very large field which virtually fills Bush Valley. For all its close proximity to the Medway Towns and M2, this is a surprisingly peaceful valley. The way descends slightly right ahead through the field towards a woodland spur, then cuts along its right-hand edge. Coming to the field corner veer left through a patch of woodland and out to a very attractive collection of houses at **Upper Bush**. (Note another NDW milestone on the left.) Wander down the lane, and when it curves left take the right-hand of two paths. This takes you through another large field and brings you to a narrow road on the outskirts of **Cuxton** (*refreshments*). Turn right along the lane for a few yards, then left by a garage (Grid ref: 701672).

Note: *For refreshments continue along the lane for about ¾ mile to* The White Hart *pub in* **Cuxton***. The village also has train services to Rochester.*

An enclosed path climbs the slope, and at the top crosses a railway bridge. Over this bear right down steps into yet another large field. Cross directly ahead through another surprisingly peaceful fold of countryside, the M2 being only a mile away, but unheard and unseen from here. On the far side a track continues alongside woodland, and up the slope you maintain direction where it forks, soon passing a memorial seat with a view through the Medway Gap. At the top of the hill gain another view to the right along the Medway's industrial reaches. Then the track curves left and right and takes you through more fields well to the right of the **Ranscombe** farm complex.

Turn right on a very narrow farm road and follow this down to a view of the Medway and a first sighting of the Medway Bridge. On coming to the A228 bear left, cross with care to the right-hand side at a junction, and where the A228 crosses the M2 turn right on a tarmac path leading onto the Medway Bridge (Grid ref: 720676).

Note: *If you intend to spend a night in* **Rochester**[3] *cross the bridge as described in the next section, and on the east side descend to a road where you turn left beneath the bridge. This leads directly into Rochester – about 1¾ miles.*

Items of Interest:

1: Trosley Country Park consists of 160 acres of wooded downland with nature trails, circular walks and some very fine viewpoints. There's a Visitor Centre with refreshment kiosk in the car park, and the Park is managed by Kent County Council.

2: The Wealdway stretches for 82 miles (132km) from Gravesend on the Kentish bank of the Thames to Beachy Head near Eastbourne. On the way it crosses the North Downs east of Trosley Country Park, then cuts through the Weald before reaching the River Medway, which it follows into Tonbridge. Thereafter the Wealdway crosses a series of High Weald ridges, makes a traverse of Ashdown Forest in East Sussex, and continues through the Low Weald to the South Downs and the spectacular clifftop finale on Beachy Head. (See *The Wealdway & The Vanguard Way* by Kev Reynolds [Cicerone].)

3: Rochester is dominated by the Norman castle that stands on high ground to guard the Medway's estuary. The outer walls were built in 1087, and the massive keep added in 1127. But long before the Norman invasion, Belgic tribes settled here, and after them the Romans fortified their camp with a wall that encased a town of 23½ acres. Saxon succeeded Roman, and they replaced the bridge across the Medway with one of their own, and also added to the town's fortifications. But it was William the Conqueror's own architect, Bishop Gundulph, who made Rochester what it is today, by designing both castle keep and the cathedral which stands in its shadow. In the 19th century Charles Dickens immortalised the town in several of his novels, variously calling it Dullborough and Cloisterham. Though born in Portsmouth (in 1812), he came to Chatham as a child when his father was employed in the Royal Navy Pay Office, and lived the rest of his life in the neighbourhood. After his death at Gads Hill near Higham in 1870, the Swiss-style chalet in which he did much of his writing was moved to Rochester where it now forms part of the Dickens Museum. Rochester holds an annual Dickens Festival, when enthusiasts converge on the town dressed as an assortment of characters from his much-loved books.

SECTION 7: THE MEDWAY TO DETLING

Distance:	**10 miles (16km)**
Maps:	**Harveys North Downs Way East 1:40,000**
	OS Landranger 178 The Thames Estuary and 188 Maidstone & The Weald of Kent 1:50,000
	OS Explorer 148 Maidstone & The Medway Towns 1:25,000
Accommodation:	**Wouldham (+ ¾ mile), Aylesford (+ 1½ miles), Boxley (+ 1 mile)**
Refreshments:	**The Robin Hood pub on Burham Common, Blue Bell Hill, Detling**

The Medway has created the largest break in the downland wall, and it is to the east of the river that the North Downs begin their arc towards the Channel. As the North Downs Way progresses along that wall, so it overlooks orchards that gave the Weald its epithet of the Garden of England – but that is for future stages. On this particular walk to Detling, the way rises steadily, with the Medway below seen twisting through a valley that combines agriculture and industry, while the Weald stretches far off as a blue misted expanse of wood, meadow and arable farmland. A long metalled section carries the walk from Wouldham Common to Blue Bell Hill, and it is from the latter that one of the most expansive views of all can be enjoyed. Below this viewpoint stands the Neolithic structure of Kits Coty House, and below that lie other Neolithic remains – Little Kits Coty and the White Horse Stone. On the Downs again, the Way passes through yet more woodland before coming to Detling Hill north-east of Maidstone.

The Medway Bridge has a span of about ¾ mile, and as you cross beside the noisy, speeding traffic on the M2, and note the High Speed

On the ascent of Box Hill, with views to the Greensand Ridge (Section 3)

The much-loved viewpoint of Box Hill above Dorking (Section 3)

Otford duckpond, the only such 'historic building' in England (Section 5)

Kits Coty House, the finest Neolithic site on the North Downs (Section 7)

East of Detling, the way edges the crest of the Downs (Section 8)

In Wye, the North Downs Way cuts through the churchyard (Section 10)

Shakespeare Cliff provides a memorable route to Dover (Section 11)

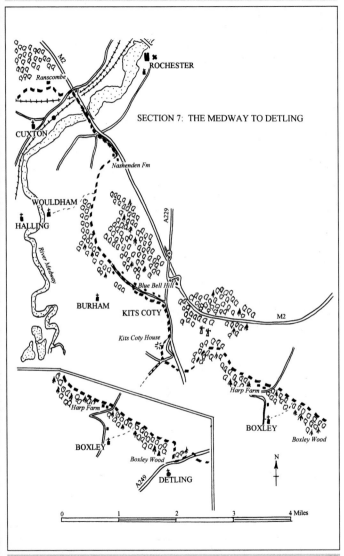

SECTION 7: THE MEDWAY TO DETLING

ROCHESTER

Ranscombe

CUXTON

Nashenden Fm

WOULDHAM

HALLING

River Medway

BURHAM

Blue Bell Hill

KITS COTY

Kits Coty House

M2

Harp Farm

BOXLEY

Harp Farm

BOXLEY

Boxley Wood

Boxley Wood

DETLING

A249

N

0   1   2   3   4 Miles

Rail Link below, it is natural to reflect on the contrast with the pace of your own journey.

To the left Rochester's cathedral and castle can be seen. Beyond these a tall power station chimney on the Isle of Grain is also evident, while to the right the view is of the river curling its way through the cut in the Downs. On the far side of the bridge the footpath slopes down to a minor road. Cross half-right into Nashenden Farm Lane – but if work on the High Speed Rail Link is in progress see below for a description of the temporary diversion.

Note: *If you intend to spend the night in* **Rochester** *turn left below the motorway bridge and follow the road through Borstal and into town where you arrive between castle and cathedral.*

Note: Temporary Diversion Route: *Do not turn into Nashenden Farm Lane, but take the next turning on the left – Burham Road. This soon leads alongside the fenced perimeter of the Rail Link construction site, but when the fencing ends you turn left to follow a cinder path as far as the next fence corner. Here you rejoin the official NDW and turn right, then up the left-hand edge of a large sloping field (Grid ref: 729657).*

Walk down Nashenden Farm Lane for a little over ½ mile, then turn right to pass along the left-hand side of farm buildings at **Nashenden Farm**. At the time of writing it is not known whether there will be a bridge across the railway here, but the route should be obvious. It leads up a sloping field, soon along the left-hand edge of a large field at the top of which you gain a fine view back to the Medway Bridge, and ahead along the river valley to the open spaces of the Weald. The path is also used by the Medway Valley Walk.[1]

This becomes a very pleasant walk, the path being long and straight and with open views for some way. But eventually it goes through a strip of woodland and brings you onto a stony, hedge-lined track, Hill Road, where you maintain direction to cross Wouldham Common.

Note: *For accommodation in* **Wouldham,** *on coming to the stony track turn right and descend to the village.*

After about ¾ mile pass the drive to Keeper's Lodge on the right. In another ¼ mile or so are the barns of Burham Hill Farm on the left.

The track now becomes a narrow metalled lane, Common Road, and passes a bungalow. About ¼ mile beyond this another lane cuts left to the *Robin Hood* pub, but you continue ahead and in another ¼ mile come to a large house on the right, aptly named Fair View, for it stands on the lip of the Downs overlooking the Medway Valley. Beyond this house you come to bungalows on the left of the road, and just past these a NDW signpost directs the way to the right through a gap in the hedge where a big open view is revealed across the Medway to the western line of the North Downs (Grid ref: 741623).

Go down the slope a few paces, then veer left and shortly come to **Blue Bell Hill** car park and picnic site.[2] The North Downs Way passes just below the car park and enters an area of trees and scrub to reach a tarmac crossing path. Descend on this below the A229. The Way then cuts across the hillside above a large farm complex, and brings you down to a road below the dual carriageway. Walk ahead, but just before the road feeds onto the dual carriageway, take a path on the right which then goes alongside another road beneath a footbridge. When you draw level with a No Entry road, turn right and descend a few concrete steps. A finger post gives the direction to Kits Coty House. The continuing path is almost tunnelled by trees, but note as you slope down that on the right, just inside an open meadow, you can visit the Neolithic upright sarsen stones known as **Kits Coty House**.[3]

At the foot of the slope is a junction of roads where you bear left and cross to a narrow byway path marked as The Pilgrims Way. (A short distance down the road another Neolithic burial site is known as Little Kits Coty, or The Countless Stones.)

Note: *For accommodation in **Aylesford** continue down the road beyond Little Kits Coty.*

As you set off along the Pilgrims Way path, be warned that it can be very wet in places after rain – at one point on my most recent walk along it, a large unavoidable puddle was deep enough to cover the tops of my boots. The way eventually curves left up a slope and joins a narrow road where you turn left. About 20 yards later turn right to pass beneath the A229, then up to a filling station and bear left.

Note: Temporary Diversion Route: *Once again the High Speed Rail Link intrudes upon the North Downs Way, and having turned left by the filling station you are then directed onto a road which goes south alongside the perimeter fence of the rail workings. At the end of the fenced area, turn left on another cinder path which takes you round the outer edge of the works, and eventually come to the continuing NDW where you turn right between two lines of trees (Grid ref: 753603) and shortly pass the White Horse Stone on the left.*

The official North Downs Way, having turned left by the filling station, is soon flanked by trees and, rising gently, passes the White Horse Stone[4] on the left. Not long after this the way breaks to the left up steps and continues to rise through Westfield Wood. (The Kent Trust for Nature Conservation maintains a nature reserve here.) When the path forks bear right, climbing the wooded slope with the aid of steps where the gradient is at its steepest. At the head of the slope in a glade of yew trees note another of the NDW milestones left of the path. This one shows you have walked 79 miles since Farnham, but with 46 miles to go before you reach Dover, or 34 to Canterbury.

Leave Westfield Wood by some standing stones (thought to have been taken from another prehistoric remains, and put here to form a gateway) and turn right along the edge of a large field. Follow the woodland until, about 50 yards beyond an electricity pylon, you turn right into the woods, then at a fork bear left. Contour the hillside just inside the woods for a little under ½ mile, then veer left at another fork, up the slope and into the corner of a small plantation. A farm track leads straight ahead, then curves right towards **Harp Farm** to reach Harp Farm Road (Grid ref: 774600).

Cross directly ahead along the right-hand side of a large field which stretches across the top of the open Downs. On the far side come to another road and bear right for a few paces, then left on a bridleway into **Boxley Wood** where a broad track leads ahead, keeping close to the left-hand edge. This is followed for more than a mile.

Note: *After about a third of a mile a path cuts off to the right – the Maidstone Centenary Walk – and descends the wooded slope to cross a narrow lane, the Pilgrims Way. The path continues over fields to **Boxley** for accommodation and/or refreshments.*

As the Way progresses, so the track narrows and eventually takes you out of the wood where the way is flanked by elder and patches of scrub. Going through a bridle gate come to a crossing byway/track and turn right. A short way down the slope the track curves right, at which point you leave it for a footpath. Over a stile veer half right across a small paddock. A gate then leads the way across a hilltop paddock and over two more stiles, the last of which is on the lip of the Downs. Descend a steep grass path into more woods, and continue under dark yew trees before arriving beside the A249 just above **Detling** (Grid ref: 794584).

Note: *If you need refreshments – or bus to Maidstone – walk down the hill for a short distance, then cross the dual carriageway with care and follow the sign into* **Detling**. *The Cock Horse pub is a short way along the road into the village. Detling also has a Post Office Stores, and bus connections with Maidstone.*

Items of Interest:

1: The Medway Valley Walk traces the course of Kent's major river for 34½ miles (55km) between Tonbridge and Rochester. For the greater part of its length it follows a towpath and visits many places of interest along the way. The river was long ago recognised for its potential as a commercial waterway, and barges journeyed inland as far as Tonbridge. There were plans to extend the navigation to Penshurst, but although work began in the 19th century, it was abandoned before reaching Leigh. Between Maidstone and Rochester the river flows past major paper factories and cement works at Snodland. (See *Medway Valley Walk* by Kev Reynolds, Annie Hood and Harold Eagles [Kent County Council].)

2: Blue Bell Hill is one of the highest points of the North Downs in Kent. The picnic site is managed by KCC, and the unploughed downland nearby provides a perfect habitat for such plants as pyramidal orchid, harebell, common rock rose and milkwort. The sporadic covering of scrub and trees attracts a variety of birdlife. Spring is a good time to enjoy the songs of willow warbler, chiffchaff and whitethroat which congregate here, while many butterflies are to be seen in the summertime. A short distance along the downland slope to the west is Burham Down Nature Reserve, which is owned by Portland Cement but managed by Kent Trust for Nature Conservation.

3: Kits Coty House is the exposed remnant of a Neolithic burial chamber dating from about 3500–2800BC. It consists of three upright sarsen stones, with a huge capstone estimated to weigh about 10 tons. The burial chamber, or barrow, is thought originally to have been some 200ft (60m) long, and would have been the last resting place for one of Kent's earliest farming communities. The site is protected by iron railings – how much better if it could be left exposed on this open site overlooking the Medway Valley.

4: The White Horse Stone also marks the site of a Neolithic place of burial. A single standing stone, more than 6ft (2m) high, it is just one of several Neolithic sites in the area. As well as Kits Coty, mentioned above, is Little Kits Coty (also known as the Countless Stones) to the west – about 20 stones which formed part of a burial chamber destroyed in the 17th century.

SECTION 8: DETLING TO HARRIETSHAM

Distance:	7½ miles (12km)
Maps:	Harveys North Downs Way East 1:40,000
	OS Landranger 188 Maidstone & The Weald of Kent and 189
	Ashford & Romney Marsh 1:50,000
	OS Explorer 148 Maidstone & The Medway Towns 1:25,000
Accommodation:	Hollingbourne (+ 1 mile), Harrietsham (+ 1 mile)
Refreshments:	Pubs in Thurnham (+ ½ mile) and Hollingbourne

Some of the finest views of the walk are experienced between Detling Hill and Dover, and along this comparatively short stage the broad open aspects of the Weald are in evidence for much of the time, setting the stage for what is to come. Not long after starting out the North Downs Way skirts below the earthwork remains of Thurnham Castle, passes high above two or three small groups of buildings spaced along the course of the Pilgrims Way, and then slopes down to join that narrow lane at Hollingbourne where a pub guards the route at a minor crossroads. From here to Harrietsham (and beyond to Charing), where the North Downs Way shares the course of the Pilgrims Way, is the easiest walking of the whole route, and you can drift along with barely an uphill slope to check the pace.

Wander uphill beside the dual carriageway of the A249, and shortly before reaching the crown of Detling Hill (about 50 yards before a minor road cuts left to Bredhurst), a NDW sign directs the walk across the main road. *Cross with the utmost caution* as traffic is very fast on the downhill lane. Safely across, descend a few steps to gain a big

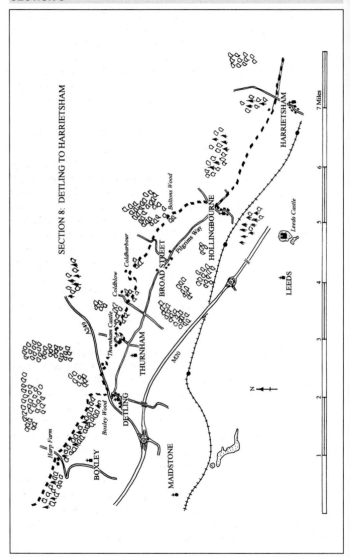

SECTION 8: DETLING TO HARRIETSHAM

view into the Weald, then over a stile bear left along a fenceline below two houses. Guided by the fence the way rounds a slope and goes down more steps to another stile. Continue ahead over the hillside towards a few steps cut into the slope beside a pair of trees. Beyond these the path rises to a fence with the houses of Thurnham seen below. Follow the fence to a narrow lane on Castle Hill (Grid ref: 807582). Turn right and wander downhill as far as a right-hand hairpin.

Note: *For refreshments continue down the lane to crossroads in* **Thurnham** *where you will find* The Black Horse *pub.*

Leave the lane on a footpath which loops round the lower edge of the steep earthworks of **Thurnham Castle**[1] partially hidden among trees. The path eases uphill and follows a fenceline on the right. When this turns left to climb the slope, go over a stile and using steps enter a belt of woodland. After descending, then rising on another flight of steps, you enter Civiley Wood. Turn right at a path junction and eventually come to the narrow Coldblow Lane which is crossed directly ahead. Maintain direction through more woods along the scarp edge. Beyond the woods the right-hand slope is fringed with trees, but these give way as you descend a slope to another panoramic view. Cross two stiles to a bridleway where you turn left into the head of a narrow coomb and once more enter woodland (Grid ref: 825578).

Before long the way forks, at which point you take the right branch, go through a gate and continue along the scarp edge. Easing through another belt of woodland there are three path junctions (one left, two right), but the NDW is well marked at each. On leaving the trees the way strikes ahead across an open slope above the few houses of Broad Street. The hillside here is part-divided by a hedge, and having passed through a gap in this, you turn left up the slope to a stile which gives onto a fence-enclosed path leading directly to a narrow road on Broad Street Hill (Grid ref: 835571).

Cross straight ahead where the continuing path goes along the top edge of an open hillside before entering **Boltons Wood** which, though part of the Hucking Estate, is owned by The Woodland Trust. On reaching a stony crossing bridleway[2] follow this up the slope to a noticeboard at another path junction. Turn right and wander along the woodland's upper edge, crossing a track immediately beneath power cables and, out of the woods, continue through a belt of scrub to a kissing gate. Here you emerge onto the crest of the Downs to a splendid, expansive view which includes oast houses and Hollingbourne church ahead.

Curving left go through a second kissing gate where the path continues between fences. A third kissing gate brings you to an open slope. Wander ahead, through a patch of scrub to a field gate with yet another kissing gate beside it. Remain along the upper edge of the slope guided by marker posts. After curving left a waymark directs you down towards Hollingbourne. At the foot of the slope continue on the left-hand edge of a large field, then onto a road which shortly leads to a minor crossroads in **Hollingbourne**[3] (Grid ref: 845554) (*refreshments, accommodation, and bus and train services to Maidstone*).

Turn left by *The Dirty Habit* pub along the narrow metalled Pilgrims Way (NDW noticeboard by the pub). When the metalled lane ends maintain direction on a track which remains at the foot of the Downs, alongside large arable fields. Although there are several track and footpath junctions, the route of the North Downs Way/Pilgrims Way is obvious, and often indicated by either concrete markers or oak posts. As the way progresses so it narrows to a footpath between hedges and trees, eventually coming alongside the garden boundary of The Dutch House[4] – a large white building. Here you come onto a metalled lane once more which leads to a crossing road above **Harrietsham** (Grid ref: 875535).

Note: *For accommodation, refreshments, and bus or train services, walk down the road to the right for about 1 mile.*

Items of interest:

1: Thurnham Castle must have been impressive in its heyday, perched as it was on the brink of the Downs. Although only fragments of curtain wall remain, and much is overgrown, the site is typical of the motte and bailey strongholds that were a feature of the southern counties before the Norman Conquest. The motte is thought to have been more than 100ft (30m) high (see *Memorials of Old Kent* by Harold Sands), which would have given this castle a commanding prospect over Maidstone and the Weald. Old accounts suggest that it was built by a Saxon named Godardus on the site of a Roman watchtower. In fact the remains of a Roman Villa were discovered nearby during road widening.

2: The bridleway in Boltons Wood is an old droveway which formerly crossed the Downs between Hucking and Hollingbourne.

3: Hollingbourne is an attractive two-part village, with several fine houses and a church containing memorials to the celebrated Culpeper family. It is said that a certain Nicholas Wood once lived here, a man with a powerful eating disorder: 'He would devour at one meal what was provided for twenty men, eat a whole hog at a sitting, and at another time thirty dozen of pigeons… this painful man spent all his estate to provide provant for his belly, and died very poor about the year 1630.'

4: The Dutch House stands near the site of an Anglo-Saxon burial mound found to contain, alongside several skeletons, a bronze bracelet and glass beads.

SECTION 9: HARRIETSHAM TO BOUGHTON LEES

Distance:	**11 miles (17½km)**
Maps:	**Harveys North Downs Way East 1:40,000**
	OS Landranger 189 Ashford & Romney Marsh 1:50,000
	OS Explorer 137 Ashford, Headcorn, Chilham & Wye 1:25,000
Accommodation:	**Charing (+ ½ mile), Westwell (+ ½ mile), and Boughton Lees**
Refreshments:	**Pubs in Charing, Westwell and Boughton Lees**

This section of the walk remains with the Pilgrims Way throughout and is, once again, an easy stretch with little height gain or loss. Charing, reached roughly halfway between Harrietsham and Boughton Lees, is worth a half-mile diversion to visit. Apart from this, there are no other settlements along the route before Boughton Lees. Even then, this is only a small village outside of which the North Downs Way divides in two: one branch veers north-east to Dover via Canterbury, the other continues directly to Wye and Dover.

Cross the road above Harrietsham, still on the metalled Pilgrims Way, and wander eastward with the large Marley Works complex glimpsed ahead. Above the lane to the left stands the impressive 18th century house known as **Stede Hill** enjoying a broad outlook to the south. After passing a few houses the lane takes you along the **Marley Works** boundary, and continues for another ¾ mile where it makes a sharp bend to the right. Now go ahead on a trackway which later narrows to a footpath and comes to another road. Continue ahead for about 150 yards, and when this road curves right by some white houses, go

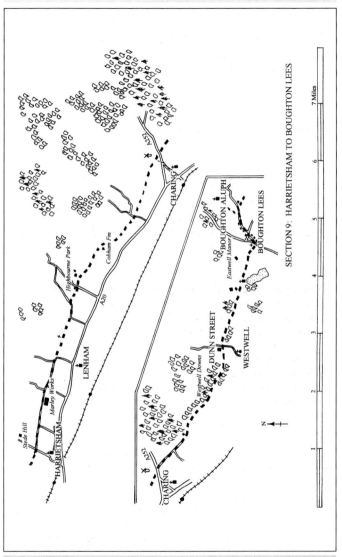

SECTION 9: HARRIETSHAM TO BOUGHTON LEES

ahead on a stony track. This soon bends as a drive towards the House
by the Cross, where you maintain direction through a field gate onto
a grass track, soon passing a chalk cross cut in the hillside to
commemorate the dead of two World Wars (Grid ref: 906527).
Immediately below the cross you'll find a seat enclosed by fencing,
the seat having been presented to the people of Lenham by the REME
Association of Ashford.[1] A NDW marker stone here informs you that
you've walked 92 miles from Farnham, and have 21 miles to go to
Canterbury, 33 to Dover.

Through another gate the way continues between hedges and
trees, and once again leads to a road at Hubbards Hill where you
bear left for about 300 yards. When the road curves left by a quarry,
break away to the right on a track at a layby. Having lost touch with
the North Downs for some time, this track takes you through scrub
along the downland slope and becomes metalled near a row of
houses. Just beyond these come to a crossing road (Rayners Hill) by
the entrance to **Highbourne Park**.[2] The continuing track takes you
half-left ahead and progresses along the edge of a vast arable field.

Pass a couple of barns at **Cobham Farm** and go ahead on a path
between open fields. Passing through two gates the way continues on
the left-hand edge of another large field where you will notice several
sarsen stones lying in the headland. At Hart Hill Farm you turn right
on a road for about 40 yards, then left on the NDW/Pilgrims Way
beside a long line of trees with Charing glimpsed ahead. The way is
then enclosed by hedges and trees, before becoming a track which
passes one or two houses above **Charing**[3] and brings you to the A252
(Grid ref: 958499).

Note: *For accommodation, refreshments, shops, Post Office, and
bus and train services, turn right and walk ½ mile into* **Charing**.

Cross the A252 with care, turn left and in a few paces bear right
along the metalled Pilgrims Way. Ignoring Toll Lane which turns off
after about ½ mile, maintain direction to Burnt House Farm where it
curves left and right. Shortly after this the lane ends at Beacon Hill
Quarry where the North Downs Way goes ahead as a woodland track.
When this forks, take the lower (right-hand) option along the bottom
edge of woods of oak, ash and beech clothing **Westwell Downs**. After
about ½ mile a brief clearing is met, with a wooden seat on the left –

Arthur's Seat. Near the end of the wood pass a couple of houses where the way forks. Take the left branch ahead, now a narrow metalled lane which feeds into another. Bear left and this will eventually bring you to **Dunn Street** Farm with one of the few campsites actually on the North Downs Way. Just beyond the farm entrance come to a T-junction (Grid ref: 992480).

Note: *For accommodation and/or refreshments turn right for ½ mile to* **Westwell**.

Cross the road to a stile and enter the estate of Eastwell Park. Bear left for a few paces, then right on a path/track between open fields. The way improves to a good trackway alongside a wood with the North Downs off to the left providing an attractive backing to the low-lying fields. On coming to a sign announcing No Entry to the Public, bear right through a gap in a belt of woodland, then left along the edge of more fields to a stile. When the woodland ends maintain direction through the middle of a large open field with an imposing white house overlooking it from the left. Eventually come to a tarmac drive and continue ahead. After about 70 yards note a footpath on the right which visits the derelict church of St Mary's[4] at the head of the 40 acres of Eastwell Lake.

Keep ahead on the drive which rises gently then cuts sharply to the left towards Eastwell Manor Hotel. At this bend go straight ahead through a kissing gate and along the top edge of a parkland meadow. Along here you will see an oak finger post announcing that this National Trail forms part of the E2 European Path.[5] About two-thirds of the way through this meadow a sign directs the NDW half-left to another kissing gate giving access to a drive opposite a small memorial garden. Bear right for a few paces, then go through a third kissing gate on the left, then diagonally half-right to the far corner, with the downland wall seen ahead.

Come to the A261 at **Boughton Lees** (*accommodation, refreshments, buses to Ashford and Wye*) and bear left by the modest-looking church of St Christopher, then cross over and take a minor road along the right-hand side of the triangular village green, on the far side of which stands *The Flying Horse* pub. At a minor crossroads go straight ahead on the metalled lane of the Pilgrims Way. After almost ½ mile the North Downs Way divides: take the left-hand route for the Canterbury loop; go straight ahead for the direct route to Wye and Dover.

Items of interest:

1: REME seat – this seat, set below the war memorial cross, commemorates 52 members of the Sixth Guards Tank Brigade who were killed by a flying bomb near Lenham in 1944.

2: Highbourne Park is the site of the former Lenham Chest Hospital, originally built for TB patients. The hospital was closed in the 1980s.

3: Charing was once an important staging post for travellers on the road to Canterbury, a handsome village of half-timbered or weatherboarded houses, the remains of one of the palaces of the Archbishops of Canterbury, and a church which is the successor to one that was 'consumed by fire [in 1590] to the very stones of the building, which happened from a gun discharged at a pigeon, then upon the roof of it.' Standing at the end of a side street, the old market place, the church has a fine ragstone tower built in about 1500, and lovely carved beams over the nave. Some of the pew ends are also beautifully carved with panels of flowers. Next to the church the former Archbishop's Palace has been incorporated into a farm. Visited by Henry VII in 1507, the palace was given to Henry VIII by Archbishop Cranmer in 1545, a quarter of a century after he had stayed there on his way to Calais to negotiate with Francis I in the 'Field of the Cloth of Gold' at Artois. Charing is on a bus route to Canterbury, while the railway station serves Ashford, Maidstone and London.

4: St Mary's Church, Eastwell is little more than a ruin at the northern end of Eastwell Lake, but it is said to contain the tomb of Richard Plantagenet, son of Richard III. The story of how he came to be buried here in 1550 is a romantic, possibly fictitious, one. As a lad of sixteen Richard was at the Battle of Bosworth Field when the cry went up: 'The King is dead, long live the King!' Hearing this, Richard fled and by a roundabout way came to Kent and found work as a mason on the Eastwell estate. On discovering his identity, the owner of the estate gave him permission to build himself a small house there, which he did, and where he lived quietly for over sixty years. During

Charing is worth a diversion to see

the Second World War the foundations of St Mary's Church were badly weakened, and most of the building collapsed during a storm in 1951. The house next to the church (but barely seen) dates from the late 13th century.

5: E2 European Path – the North Downs Way has been incorporated into the ultra long distance European walking network as a link with E2, the premier north–south route between the Low Countries and the Mediterranean. The UK strand covers about 870 miles (1400km) between Stranraer and Dover, joining sections of the Pennine Way, Tameside Trail, Goyt Way, Gritstone Trail, Staffordshire Way and Heart of England Way. At Bourton-on-the-Water it picks up the Oxfordshire Way, then takes the Thames Path before breaking off on the Wey Navigation and coming to the North Downs Way. Walkers intending to follow E2 as far as the Mediterranean cross the Channel to Ostend, then walk to Antwerp to join the well-known GR5 which swings across to the Vosges and down the length of the French Alps.

DIRECT ROUTE TO DOVER VIA WYE

SECTION 10: BOUGHTON LEES
TO ETCHINGHILL

Distance:	**13 miles (21km)**
Maps:	**Harveys North Downs Way East 1:40,000**
	OS Landranger 189 Ashford & Romney Marsh 1:50,000
	OS Explorer 137 Ashford, Headcorn, Chilham & Wye and
	138 Dover, Folkestone & Hythe 1:25,000
Accommodation:	**Wye, Stowting and Etchinghill**
Refreshments:	**Pubs in Wye, Stowting and Etchinghill (+ ½ mile)**

Along the direct route to Dover, the English Channel comes into view for the first time on this penultimate stage of the walk. By contrast with the previous section it is quite a demanding stretch with several steep climbs, but each one rewards either with tremendous open views or an easy level walk along the North Downs escarpment. This is sheep-grazing country, so should you be walking with a dog it is important to keep it under control.

Note: *There are only two villages actually on the route of the North Downs Way, Wye and Stowting, with two or three close by. Wye is met shortly after leaving Boughton Lees. A neat little town tucked against the Downs, it has several shops from which to buy foodstuffs for the day. Stowting only has a pub.*

Almost ½ mile north-east of the village green at Boughton Lees, a NDW signpost directs Canterbury-bound walkers to a path on the

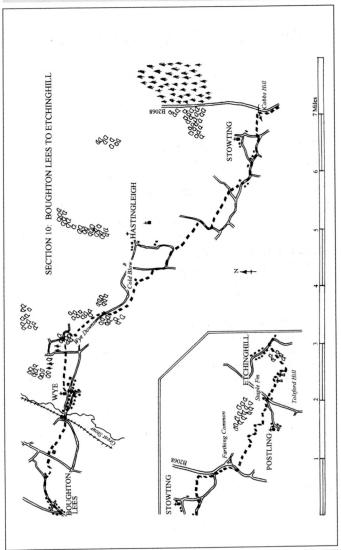

SECTION 10: BOUGHTON LEES TO ETCHINGHILL

left. The alternative direct route to Wye and Dover continues ahead along the metalled lane of the Pilgrims Way, but when it curves left shortly after, cross a stile on the right and go round the left headland of a large field. The way soon cuts right at a corner, and left at the next boundary corner. At the next left-hand angle turn right and cross the field to the A28.

Turn left for a few paces, and just beyond the entrance to Perry Court Farm, cross the road and enter orchards by a stile in the hedge. Walk down the left-hand edge, through a gap in the bottom boundary, and maintain direction along a track. When you come to the end of a small orchard on the left, turn right, then left on another track leading between fields with Wye seen ahead, and a memorial crown[1] cut in the chalk of the Downs above it. When the track swings left, go straight ahead on a footpath through two fields, to reach another road (Grid ref: 046468).

Bear left and you shortly come to a junction where you turn right and cross the railway line by the station in **Wye**.[2] Walk ahead over a bridge spanning the Great Stour River, and past the *The Tickled Trout* pub on the river bank. The road forks and you keep ahead along Bridge Street, soon passing village stores. Turn left into Church Street opposite Wye Methodist Church.

Wye has a choice of food shops, pubs, restaurants, accommodation etc. Trains serve Canterbury and Ashford, and there are buses to Chilham, Chartham, Canterbury and Ashford.

On coming to the large Parish Church of St Gregory and St Martin (foodstore on the left), enter the churchyard and take the footpath branching diagonally right. Out of the churchyard turn left between hedges and allotments, and at the end turn right. Over a crossing road continue ahead on a service road between buildings of Wye College, and maintain direction along a track which leads to a minor crossing road. A bridleway continues ahead to a gate at the foot of the Downs (Grid ref: 068469). Through the gate a chalk track climbs the wooded slope, at the head of which you bear right along a narrow lane.

When the woodland ends go up steps on the right, and after crossing two stiles turn left to walk along the lip of **Wye Downs**,[3] passing above the unseen memorial crown. Beyond a seat with a

The sign outside Boughton Lees marks the parting of the ways between the main and alternative routes

view the trail veers away from the fenceline and weaves a course among several hollows before coming to a kissing gate. Through this follow the left-hand fence until reaching a minor road where you bear right to a T-junction. Cross straight ahead to a stile giving access to Wye Downs National Nature Reserve through Pickersdane Scrubs woodland. Out of the woods bear half-right at a junction of paths, then through a metal kissing gate follow the fenceline for a few paces before branching half-left on a grass path to a waymark post. Here go half-right. Pass above a seat and wander ahead parallel with the right-hand fence. Over a stile the way continues, led by fences, to a stony track by barns at **Cold Blow** (Grid ref: 086448).

I was glad to have walked this way several times before, to have enjoyed the broad panorama from the scarp edge, to have zigzagged among the cowslips and orchids of springtime, to have been romanced by the trilling of larks from a warm and cloudless sky. Good to have those memories, for today there were no views at all; visibility was limited to a dozen paces and rain was bouncing on the cropped turf, lying in pools wherever a natural saucer occurred in the grass. Sheep were spooked by my appearance, their sodden wool turned grey by the foul weather. Drifting in a sullen line they were a scene of utter dejection. 'Just be thankful it's not winter,' I told them, and splashed my way past through the puddles of high summer.

Across the track continue ahead until you reach the end of pastureland where you go over a stile into an arable field, then cut half-left to a road. Turn right and after ¼ mile bear left at a junction, in the direction of South Hill. After almost ½ mile the road bends sharply to the left, at which point leave it and go straight ahead on a hedge-lined track between fields. (In wet weather this track becomes heavily waterlogged.) Eventually come to a narrow road and turn right, soon returning to the scarp edge near a trig point on Brabourne Downs. The road curves left and slopes downhill. As it bends to the right, cut left through a gate and proceed along a track. When it forks take the right branch alongside a fence, through a second gate and ahead beside Long Wood. The track soon narrows to footpath dimensions and, reaching a minor road (Brabourne Lane), crosses straight ahead to become a pleasant tree-lined track sloping downhill to another road (Grid ref: 113417).

Bear left, and when the road forks by a telephone kiosk on the edge of **Stowting** (*accommodation, refreshments*), take the left branch. About 120 yards later the official North Downs Way mounts steps on the right and enters a paddock. It then works a way through a succession of small paddocks connected by stiles before returning to the road again opposite *The Tiger Inn*. You may find it preferable to ignore this paddock section and remain on the road. Just beyond the pub bear left at another road junction and continue beside a wood. The road then curves to the right, passes the entrance to Water Farm and, very narrow now, rises between banks and hedges. Take the second footpath on the left – a narrow sunken path going uphill among trees – to another lane. Cross directly ahead into a downland meadow which you ascend on its right-hand edge, soon gaining very fine views over the surrounding country.

At the head of the slope cross two stiles in succession, and proceed over **Cobbs Hill** parallel with the left-hand fence. On the far side of the field there's a gap with a stile on the right. Over this walk round the left headland of another field, keeping within the field at the next corner, now with the B2068 (a Roman road) on the far side of the boundary hedge. About 20 yards to the right of the next field corner cross a stile onto a lane, and continue along the left-hand edge of the next field ahead. Remaining parallel with the road look for another stile on the left near a line of tall trees. Over this stile a few steps lead up to the road (Grid ref: 135402).

On the opposite side come onto a footpath between fields. This soon has a hedge and fence boundary on the left, and before long you cross a stile and descend through a dry valley. In the bed of this coomb the way leads past a couple of ash tees and beside a fence to a waymark post directing you left into a narrow grass gully, at the head of which you come to a fence and turn right. Now follow the fenceline as it contours along the crest with views onto Postling[4] – a trim-looking village snug at the foot of the slope.

In a 'bay' of hillside the slope has formed several terraces. Take the middle one and come to a marker post which sends you up again to cross a stile on the ridge-line. Keep to the right-hand edge of a field to another stile, turn right and descend steeply. Halfway down the slope bear left and wander ahead as far as a field gate and a stile. Over this go down the right-hand side of a meadow, and on reaching the corner bear left, parallel with a sunken lane. Keep alongside the boundary, but on reaching the far corner by **Staple Farm**, go out to a Y-shaped road junction.

Cross a little to the right, then almost immediately take a path on the left among trees. Ascend the right-hand edge of a sloping meadow towards the mast of Swingfield Radio Station. The North Downs Way skirts the left-hand perimeter fence, then crosses a stile on the right to go round a second fence leading to the entrance drive. Across the drive a stile gives access to a meadow where you walk along the left-hand side through an avenue of hawthorn trees. (This path is shared by the Saxon Shore Way and Elham Valley Way.[5]) The meadow here is occasionally used as a training ground by the Ministry of Defence.

Over a stile by a field gate continue with glimpsed views to Summerhouse Hill to the south, then along the edge of woodland

and the meadows that lie beyond it, sloping down to a road on the outskirts of **Etchinghill** (Grid ref: 169392).

> **Note:** *For refreshments turn left into **Etchinghill** for The New Inn. The village is on a bus route between Canterbury and Folkestone. It also has b&b accommodation.*

Items of interest:

1: Wye Memorial Crown – cut into the chalk of the downland wall directly above Wye, the crown commemorates the coronation of Edward VII in 1902, and is one of just 25 hill carvings left in England.

2: Wye is an old market town ('a pratie market townelet' according to Leland), noted for its agricultural college. The original seminary college for priests was founded in 1432 by Cardinal John Kempe, Archbishop of Canterbury who was born in the town in 1380, but this was dissolved in 1545 and taken over as a grammar school. In 1894 the buildings were adapted for use as an agricultural college, and in 1900 the college became a faculty of London University. The church of St Gregory and St Martin dates from the 12th and early 13th centuries, but was enlarged 200 years later by Kempe. In 1572 it was damaged by lightning, and the tower collapsed following an earth tremor in 1686. The Stour Valley Walk passes through Wye on its 51 mile (82km) journey between Lenham and Sandwich Bay. See *Stour Valley Walk* by Veronica Litten (Kent County Council).

3: Wye Downs provide some of the finest panoramic views of the entire North Downs. A fertile chequerboard of fields and meadows is seen spread out below, wound about with ribbon-like lanes and dotted with farms and small hamlets; in the distance the glimmer of the English Channel. It was on these Downs that the North Downs Way was officially opened by the then Archbishop of Canterbury, Dr Donald Coggan, in 1978. Wye Downs National Nature Reserve stretches for 1½ miles along the scarp face. Established in 1961 it claims a wide range of plants and wildlife, including some 27 species of butterfly and 90 birds. Orchids are common, and no less than 17 species have been identified here. Along the Downs the Devil's Kneading Trough is one of several steep-sided coombs moulded by melt-water from the retreating snows of the last Ice Age, about 10,000 years ago.

4: Postling is a very small village in orchard country, the one-time home of novelist Joseph Conrad, where he wrote *Lord Jim*.

5: The Saxon Shore Way and Elham Valley Way are both met at various times in the closing stages of the walk. The SSW is a well-established long-distance route of 163 miles (262km) that begins on the bank of the Thames at Gravesend, and links a number of coastal defences built by the Romans against Saxon raiding parties, before ending at Hastings. See *The Saxon Shore Way* by Bea Cowan (Aurum Press). The Elham Valley Way is less ambitious, but it goes through some very fine country between Canterbury and Hythe – a walk of 23 miles (37km). See *Elham Valley Way* by Brian Hart (Kent County Council).

SECTION 11: ETCHINGHILL TO DOVER

Distance:	**11½ miles (18½km)**
Maps:	**Harveys North Downs Way East 1:40,000**
	OS Landranger 179 Canterbury & East Kent 1:50,000
	OS Explorer 138 Dover, Folkestone & Hythe 1:25,000
Accommodation:	**Arpinge (+ ½ mile), Folkestone (+ 2 miles), Capel-le-Ferne and Dover**
Refreshments:	**Pubs at Capel-le-Ferne and in Dover, cafés near Capel and Dover**

The long trail from Farnham comes to a fitting conclusion along the clifftop walk overlooking the Straits of Dover, but this final stage is a demanding one with steep ascents and descents, and a surprisingly long stretch with a sense of remoteness to it – despite the proximity of a major road and rail carrying traffic bound for the Channel Tunnel. With careful planning the National Trail skirts to the north of Folkestone over the summits of prominent hills. It passes an impressive Battle of Britain Memorial, works round the sombre fortifications of the Western Heights and finishes in view of Dover Castle, one of the great fortresses of southern England. There are lovely areas of countryside to enjoy, though the walk also looks down on the Channel Tunnel Terminal, and the curious man-made Samphire Hoe Country Park below Shakespeare Cliff, created on the chalk spoil from the Chunnel left at the foot of this treasured stretch of Heritage Coast. Striding across Shakespeare Cliff with the sea lapping far below, both the castle and busy harbour of Dover come into view as beacons to guide the final miles.

On the outskirts of Etchinghill the North Downs Way turns right on the road, but in a few paces forks left down a minor dead-end road

SECTION 11: ETCHINGHILL TO DOVER

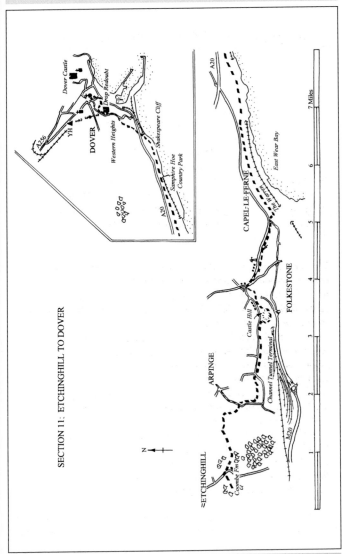

towards **Coombe Farm**. At the farm entrance bear left by some bollards, then half-right down a lovely sloping meadow to a woodland corner. A path leads through the woods, crossing a footbridge over a stream and branching left at a fork to pass beneath a railway bridge which, from 1889 to 1947, carried trains between Canterbury and Folkestone. Cut across a field to a belt of trees where you curve right at the foot of a steep slope into a very narrow dry valley. The path goes to its head, then bears right along a fenceline, from which views south-west show the distinctive domed shape of Summerhouse Hill.

The way follows fences round several interlinking meadows until it comes to a bridleway near Shearins Bungalow (Grid ref: 185394). Turn right and walk along the bridleway as far as a narrow lane.

Note: *For accommodation in* **Arpinge** *turn left along the lane for about ½ mile.*

Across the lane go over a stile and turn right along the edge of a large open field, gaining a view of the extensive marshalling yards of the Channel Tunnel.[1] Coming to a kissing gate on the right you join a clear trail across Northcliffe. (A NDW milestone gives Farnham as 115 miles, Dover 15 and Canterbury 27 miles from here.) Through a second kissing gate the path curves slightly left into what was once Peene Quarry,[2] then up steps and through a final kissing gate.

The way continues across Danton Lane, the path now running parallel with the lane across Cheriton Hill directly above the hideous marshalling yards, with Cheriton spread out beyond that, and then the Channel gleaming towards France. For some way the path goes through interlinking meadows before passing along the edge of a steep woodland and coming onto the lane. Immediately turn right onto a path which loops round the south side of **Castle Hill**,[3] below which the Channel Tunnel burrows into the Downs.

Round the earthworks the path forks. Bear left, then curve right to leave Castle Hill by following a fenceline. Below to the right the A20 can be seen entering a tunnel cut into Round Hill. The path curves away from the fence to go through a kissing gate near a row of bungalows, and through a second kissing gate it then climbs over Round Hill and descends on the far side to the A260 Canterbury Road (Grid ref: 222385).

Cross to Crete Road East and wander along it until a sign directs the North Downs Way into the right-hand meadow where you then walk parallel with the road across Creteway Down overlooking Folkestone and the English Channel. Cross another minor road and, regaining meadowland, maintain direction across gorse-covered Dover Hill, passing a Second World War pillbox and a trig point beyond that, finally coming out near the end of Crete Road East at the B2011 near *The Valiant Sailor* pub. Take a footpath alongside the pub.

Note: *For accommodation break away from the path where it forks at a corner, and descend to* **Folkestone**.

The path of the North Downs Way edges a caravan park and emerges onto the open Downs once more, with Folkestone now behind you and the White Cliffs of Dover in view ahead. There follows a splendid walk across the clifftop, passing to the right of a very fine Battle of Britain Memorial – a contemplative airman in stone, gazing south across the Channel. Keep well to the right of this and continue along the cliff edge, soon descending a steep flight of steps, then climbing another flight immediately after. Turn left at a concrete drive, then up a footpath on the right where the way passes the end of a row of gardens – the French coast is often in view from here.

Come to the *Clifftop Café* where an alternative path descends to **The Warren**,[4] but the way continues above the café, parallel with a road through **Capel-Le-Ferne** (*accommodation, refreshments*), eventually veering away from the cliff edge and coming to a junction of drives. Bear right on the drive/track signposted to Abbots Cliffe House. The stony track progresses for some way across the cliffs, passing as it does a curious upright concrete structure (an experimental radar reflector) with a concave dish on its seaward side. On the next rise go through a gate and veer half-right on a footpath towards a railway tunnel air shaft.

The path winds over **Shakespeare Cliff** above Samphire Hoe Country Park[5] passing a number of wartime bunkers as a reminder that this coastline has often been under threat of invasion. It is from here that Dover comes into view for the first time. A steep descent brings you to the last official milestone of the North Downs Way (122 miles to Farnham, 2 to Dover, 20 to Canterbury), while the final descent from the cliffs is on a concrete footpath beside allotments leading to an underpass beneath the A20 on the outskirts of **Dover** (Grid ref: 309400).

On the north side of the A20 bear right, then left into King Lear's Way, a residential street. Curve right into the Ropewalk, and at the end of the close ascend a path on the left to a kissing gate through which a trail rises through a meadow, and eventually brings you onto a stony track leading to a road. Keep ahead along this to pass the remains of a small medieval church built by the Knights Templar in 1128. At a T-junction turn left, and after passing the Grand Shaft, as the road curves right look for a finger post on the right directing the way towards the Drop Redoubt. Here you climb a flight of steps, go through a kissing gate and wander across a high meadow overlooking Dover Priory Station. The path takes you alongside the Redoubt, part of Dover's defensive system known as the **Western Heights**[6] and makes a partial loop round it. The Redoubt is a tremendous vantage point, and after admiring the view over the town, you turn left by another kissing gate and descend to a broad flight of steps which take you down to a road where you turn right and then curve to the left (Adrian Street). At the busy A256 turn left and cross the road via a pedestrian crossing near the White Cliffs Experience. Wander down Queen Street, then left into King Street which leads directly to the Market Square and the end of the North Downs Way (Grid ref: 319414).

Note: *If you plan to stay overnight at the **youth hostel**, leave the Market Square by heading left to the A256, and there turn right, soon reaching London Road (still the A256). The youth hostel is number 306, and it stands on the left-hand side of the road. (See YHA Handbook for booking details.)*

Dover (*accommodation, refreshments*) has no shortage of hotels, guest houses, b&b and a youth hostel. As the 'Gateway to England' the town has faced the threat of invasion more often than any other in Britain, hence the impressive array of fortifications – not only the massive castle, but those of the Western Heights too. Iron Age settlers built primitive earthwork defences. The Romans turned *Dubris* into a walled city and erected two *pharos*, or lighthouses (the earliest in

Britain) here in the 1st century, while the Saxons who came after them created their own fortified town with the church of St Mary-in-Castro at its heart. But the great castle which overlooks Dover is a product of the 12th century Normans who built upon Roman foundations. The keep stands 465ft (142m) above the sea and is 91ft (28m) high, its walls are 21ft (6m) thick at the base, the well descends 400ft (122m) to below street-level, and the castle was continuously garrisoned for 800 years. In 1597 it was described by the German, Paul Hentzner, as 'a very extensive castle [which] rises to a surprising height, in size like a little city, extremely well fortified, and thickset with towers, and seems to threaten the sea beneath'. (Tourist Information Centre: Burlington House, Townwall St, Dover CT16 1JR ☎ 01304 205108.)

Items of interest:

1: The Channel Tunnel was opened in 1994 following seven years of construction work and two centuries of dreams and fears. In fact a candle-lit tunnel beneath the English Channel was first discussed in 1802, and a start was made on both sides in the 1880s, and again in the 1960s. Consisting of three separate tunnels – two single-track rail tunnels for passenger trains, and a central tunnel for maintenance – the scheme was controversial from the outset. Although a remarkable engineering project, the environmental consequences are evident.

2: Peene Quarry on the sharp bend of the Downs above the Channel Tunnel Terminal buildings, is where chalk was extracted in the 16th century to build Sandgate Castle for Henry VIII.

3: Castle Hill, also known as Caesar's Camp, bears the remains of a Norman ring and bailey castle, one of the largest of its kind in the south-east of England and thought to have been built in the 12th century.

4: The Warren, or Folkestone Warren, is an interesting but unstable area of the lower cliffs formed by a number of landslips that have occurred during the last 4000 years. The base Gault clay has been overlaid by chalk, causing the slips. In 1915 a major landslip here blocked the railway which runs between the cliffs and the shoreline from Folkestone to Dover. Earlier, in 1843, about 185 barrels of gunpowder were used to demolish a section of cliffs north-east of The Warren, in order to lay the railway line.

5: Samphire Hoe Country Park below Shakespeare Cliff was created from 5 million (of nearly 7 million) cubic metres of chalk spoil dug from the Channel bed while tunnelling to France. The dump of Chalk Marl was held by a new sea wall, then landscaped and sown with grasses and wild flowers spreading away from buildings that contain part of the tunnel's ventilation system. The name 'Samphire Hoe' comes from the local rock samphire mentioned by Edgar in Shakespeare's *King Lear*: 'There is a cliff, whose high and bending head / Looks fearfully in the confinéd deep... / How fearful / And dizzy 'tis to cast one's eyes so low! / The crows and choughs that wing the midway air / Show scarce so gross as beetles; half way down / Hangs one that gathers samphire, dreadful trade!' Managed by the White Cliffs Countryside Project, the Country Park is open daily from 7am until dusk.

6: The Western Heights which include the Drop Redoubt and Grand Shaft, form a key part of Dover's defence system. Work started on the fortification of the hill in 1793 at the onset of the Napoleonic War, was interrupted in 1814 following the Treaty of Paris, and completed in 1853. The defences consist of a labyrinth of brick chambers and galleries, huge walls and tunnels, and ditches 30ft (9m) wide. In the Grand Shaft three interlocking spiral staircases wind down through a brick shaft to a tunnel which leads out to Snargate Street. The sheer quantity of bricks used in these defences caused William Cobbett to complain that they could have built a cottage for every labourer in Kent and Sussex. 'Either madness the most humiliating, or profligacy the most scandalous must have been at work here for years,' he blustered.

Canterbury Cathedral (Section 10a)

Chilham's Jacobean castle, set back from the village square (Section 10a)

The open farmland of the inner Downs near Womenswold (Section 11a)

BOUGHTON LEES TO DOVER VIA THE CANTERBURY LOOP

SECTION 10(a): BOUGHTON LEES TO CANTERBURY

Distance:	13 miles (21km)
Maps:	Harveys North Downs Way East 1:40,000
	OS Landranger 179 Canterbury & East Kent 1:50,000
	OS Explorer 137 Ashford, Headcorn, Chilham & Wye,
	149 Sittingbourne & Faversham, and 150 Canterbury & The Isle of Thanet 1:25,000
Accommodation:	Chilham, Chartham Hatch, Harbledown and Canterbury
Refreshments:	Chilham, Old Wives Lees, Chartham Hatch and Canterbury

The Canterbury loop to Dover is every bit as scenically interesting and varied as the more direct route, and has in addition the historic and architectural enhancement of England's premier cathedral city as a significant lure. Much smaller but no less charming, the lovely village of Chilham is also visited. In fact this section of the walk goes through more villages than on any recent stage, as well as lengthy periods with barely a house in sight.

On the way to Canterbury the walk remains on the west side of the Great Stour's valley throughout. This river forces the last major break in the downland wall, a break that is evident as you climb onto the Downs once more beyond Boughton Aluph and gaze south and east to the misty blue flank of the eastern Downs that arcs as a backdrop

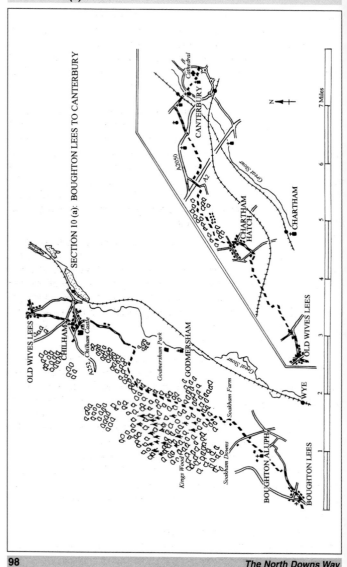

SECTION 10 (a): BOUGHTON LEES TO CANTERBURY

The North Downs Way

to Wye. Beyond Boughton Aluph the North Downs Way strikes through King's Wood above Godmersham Park, used by Jane Austen in some of her novels, then enters Chilham by the 'back door' so to speak. As one of Kent's most attractive villages, Chilham is worth exploring before pushing on through Old Wives Lees into the orchard country that leads at last to Canterbury and its glorious cathedral.

On the country road of the Pilgrims Way about ½ mile north-east of the village green at Boughton Lees, turn left on a signposted footpath which goes between fences and a veritable tunnel of trees to a view of Boughton Aluph's stumpy church tower directly ahead. There's not much to **Boughton Aluph**, other than a church, manor and farm, but with the backing of the North Downs it has a pleasing effect. The path cuts along the right-hand side of the churchyard, where All Saints Church,[1] though looking quaint, fails to give more than a vague hint that it might be worth straying into.

Cross a drive by the churchyard entrance and over a stile continue ahead through a meadow to another stile in the far left-hand corner. Maintain direction through a large open field with views east across the Stour Valley to Wye Downs. On reaching the far side of the field the path is led between hedges and out to a country road, which you cross directly ahead onto a track leading to **Soakham Farm** (b&b when passed on research). Views are still very fine across the valley, and ahead to the wood-crowned Soakham Downs.

Pass the farmhouse on your left and remain on the track which now rises steadily. At a field gate turn right on a footpath sloping uphill. It veers left, still rising, and at the head of the slope you cross a track and veer half-right into the extensive **King's Wood**[2] (Grid ref: 040495). Coming to a four-way crossing track take the right-hand option, and when it forks just beyond, take the left branch through a coppiced area. Sloping downhill continue ahead, ignoring a broad ride on the left and a path cutting right, but at the next fork the North Downs Way branches left on a path/track. As the way progresses it draws close to the woodland edge with occasional views across the Stour Valley. Below here lies Godmersham Park,[3] once the home of Jane Austen's brother.

At the next junction continue ahead to pass another NDW milestone announcing 103 miles to Farnham, 10 to Canterbury, 28 to

Cottages in Chilham, an attractive village six miles from Canterbury

Dover. The path remains in the wood with prominent waymarks at junctions until coming to a gate and a crossing track where you turn right and shortly emerge from the woods. The track now slopes downhill with a panoramic view of the Stour Valley, and the red-brick mansion of Godmersham Park seen to the right. At the foot of the slope turn left and come onto a minor road, Mountain Street. In a little over a mile, and after passing some very attractive half-timbered houses, the road leads to School Hill, at the top of which you enter the village square of **Chilham**[4] (*accommodation, refreshments*) (Grid ref: 068535).

Cross to the churchyard of St Mary's, which you enter beside a 15th century pub, *The White Horse*. Immediately after passing the west door of the church veer slightly left and descend a faint grass path among trees to come onto a narrow lane which in turn leads to the A252. Cross directly ahead to a minor road, direction Selling. At crossroads again continue ahead for a little over ½ mile to **Old Wives**

Lees where you come to a multi-junction crossroads. Half-right ahead walk along Lower Lees Road, which once more is on the course of the Pilgrims Way. A short distance along here you will pass the village Post Office which also serves as a general store.

After passing a converted oast house, just under ½ mile from the crossroads, turn left at a junction, and a few paces later at the next junction turn right, then almost immediately go left through a kissing gate onto a tree-lined path between orchards – a fine windbreak avenue. When the left-hand orchard ends it is replaced by a coppiced woodland, and at the end of the trees you walk ahead along the left-hand edge of a hop garden, then turn right on a crossing track (Grid ref: 084554). In a few paces bear left to ascend a slope alongside a row of beech trees. Near the head of the slope a simple bench seat entices you to rest for a moment to enjoy a charming landscape of folding Downs dressed with orchards, hop gardens and white-tipped oasts.

Beyond the beech trees continue to a field corner, then bear left for about 200 yards where you then cross a stile on your right and walk down the left-hand edge of an orchard. The way continues through an extensive area of orchards, bringing you onto a track where you bear right, then left. At a junction of tracks in a dip go ahead uphill for a few paces, then left to cross the Faversham–Canterbury railway line.

Over the railway turn right on a track which takes you into more orchards. Cross a lane just to the right of The Barn Oast and maintain direction on a footpath rising alongside Fright Wood. On coming to a crossing concrete farm road bear left through yet more orchards. When the farm road turns abruptly to the left at a fork, go ahead towards oast houses. Turn left in front of a green Dutch barn, then right on a gravel drive through a private garden to a country road. Turn left, then right into New Town Street, which leads to **Chartham Hatch** (*accommodation, refreshments*).

At a T-junction turn left into Howfield Lane, and shortly after passing Nightingale Close go along an enclosed footpath to a minor road which you cross straight ahead between bungalows, then branch right into a playing field. The way skirts the playing field and enters woods, soon sloping downhill and along the left-hand side of No

Man's Orchard.[5] The North Downs Way breaks away to the left at the end of the orchard and proceeds through a further stretch of woodland. There are several alternative paths here, but the way is obvious at each junction.

With the busy A2 seen ahead, the way bears right to gain a minor road by which you cross the A2 (Grid ref: 121578). Across the roadbridge turn right on a bridleway, and wander alongside an orchard before veering left between more orchards, then cross a footbridge spanning a small stream and go up a wooded rise to a narrow road by the entrance to Mindora Heights, the first house you come to in **Harbledown** (*accommodation, refreshments*).

Passing the National Trust-owned Golden Hill on the left, keep along Mill Lane as far as the A2050 which is reached by a roundabout from which Canterbury Cathedral can be seen to the right. Cross with care towards the *Victoria Hotel*, then bear right into London Road. (If the road is extra busy and crossing difficult, there is an underpass beneath the A2050.) Keep along London Road until you come to a T-junction by St Dunstan's Church, then turn right along St Dunstan Street. Go through the 14th century Westgate across the River Stour, and walk along the pedestrian precinct of the High Street, then left down Mercery Lane to Christ Church Gate by Canterbury Cathedral (Grid ref: 150578). (*For the* **youth hostel** *see Section 11(a)*.)

Canterbury (*accommodation, refreshments*) has all services, as befits one of England's major tourist centres. (Tourist Information Centre: 34 St Margaret's St, Canterbury CT1 2TG ☎ 01227 766567.) Historically, architecturally and culturally, the city rewards the walker passing through as well as the visitor with several days to spend exploring. Iron Age man settled there on both banks of the Stour, and later, during the Roman occupation, it was made the regional capital known as Durovernum Cantiacorum, the hub from which important roads radiated to Dover, Lympne, Richborough and Reculver. After the Romans, Canterbury became the capital of Ethelbert, a pagan king whose French wife had become a Christian, and whose chapel (built in AD 560 on Roman foundations) became St Martin's Church – England's oldest church still in use. When St Augustine arrived in 597 with 40 Christian missionaries, Ethelbert became a convert and gave Augustine land on which to build an abbey outside the city walls. The town steadily developed as an important trading centre, at the same time as its ecclestiastical foundation mushroomed. Following the murder of Thomas à Becket in 1170, Canterbury Cathedral became England's prime centre of pilgrimage, and the medieval heart of the modern city is partly a response to this pilgrimage. If you have no time to visit any other part of Canterbury before moving on towards Dover, you should at least give an hour or more to the cathedral itself. It is, quite simply, one of the most magnificent buildings in all Britain.

Items of interest:

1: All Saints Church, Boughton Aluph is thought to stand on the site of an earlier place of worship, for when the Normans came Bocton, as it was then called, had a Saxon church, seven and a half farms and two mills. In 1210 the manor was owned by Aluphus of Boctune and it is thought it was he who built the present church. Its size would suggest that the hamlet was then much bigger than it is today, but was probably depleted by the Black Death. Although the tower was damaged by incendiaries in 1940, and the church is no longer used for regular services, some say it is to be respected architecturally 'and not just loved for its picturesque qualities' (John Newman, *The Buildings of England – North East and East Kent*).

2: King's Wood is managed by the Forestry Commission, and consists of a mixture of mature beech, yew and sweet chestnut coppice. A glance at the map shows that a sweep of almost unbroken woodland stretches from Charing to Chilham, and King's Wood is by far the most extensive section.

3: Godmersham Park was bequeathed in 1794 to Jane Austen's brother Edward, who later changed his name to that of his benefactress, Mrs Catherine Knight. Jane Austen was a frequent visitor and once claimed that 'Kent is the only place for happiness, everyone is rich there.' It is said that Godmersham was used as the setting for several of her novels. Edward's grandson, who became Lord Brabourne, described it as being 'situated in one of the most beautiful parts of Kent, namely, in the valley of the Stour, which lies between Ashford and Canterbury... A little beyond the church you see the mansion… Godmersham Park, beyond the house, is upon the chalk downs, and on its further side is bounded by King's Wood, a large tract of woodland containing many hundred acres, and possessed by several different owners.'

4: Chilham is an architecturally elegant village whose written history dates from Roman times. The hilltop site of the Jacobean Chilham Castle is thought to have been the battleground on which the Britons met their Roman invaders, and 18th century excavations revealed the remains of a Roman senate house. The original castle, with Roman foundations, is recorded as having been a garrison in 1173, but in 1603 the owner, Sir Dudley Digges, commissioned the mansion whose gardens are open to the public today. The storm which swept across southern England in October 1987 severely damaged a yew tree, said to have stood in the churchyard for 1300 years in the shadow of St Mary's Church. The church itself is 700 years old, standing on the site of a much earlier place of worship. In the south-east corner of the tower is a beacon turret, octagonal in shape, which had a small steeple until 1784.

5: No Man's Orchard was originally planted in 1947, and became a community orchard in 1995 thanks to help from the Kentish Stour Countryside Project, the Parish Councils of Chartham and Harbledown, and the generosity of a number of local people. Maintenance costs of the orchard are met from the sale of apples grown there. Among the varieties are James Grieve, Worcester Pearmain, Golden Delicious and six cider apple varieties planted a year after the orchard came into local ownership.

SECTION 11(a): CANTERBURY TO SHEPHERDSWELL

Distance:	10½ miles (16½km)
Maps:	Harveys North Downs Way East 1:40,000
	OS Landranger 179 Canterbury & East Kent 1:50,000
	OS Explorer 150 Canterbury & The Isle of Thanet and 138 Dover, Folkestone & Hythe 1:25,000
Accommodation:	Bridge (+ ½ mile), Womenswold and Shepherdswell
Refreshments:	Bridge (+ ½ mile), Woolage Green (+ ½ mile), Shepherdswell

Out of Canterbury you lose any real impression of walking on the North Downs. With no scarp slope to add perspective, the nature of the walk has taken a drastic change. Across Barham Downs the North Downs Way experiences wide open spaces, but it is not until the final stage approaches Dover that the contrast of low valley and lofty Downs is restored. That is not to suggest that this section of the long walk is in any way inferior or less interesting than others, it is simply different. The walking is as enjoyable as elsewhere. As for villages passed along the way, Patrixbourne is noted for its delightful small church, Womenswold is little more than a farming hamlet, Woolage was built for colliers in the days when the East Kent coalfields were in full production, and Shepherdswell (or Sibertswold), which offers both refreshment and accommodation, has an unusual church with neither tower nor steeple, but whose bell hangs from a tree in the churchyard.

Facing Canterbury Cathedral's ornate Christ Church Gate turn right. On coming to a major crossing road (the ring road) cross, turn right then left to pass alongside the remains of St Augustine's Abbey, and continue beside the A257. Take the first turning on the right (Spring Lane), and right again along the Pilgrims Way, before veering left on a tarmac path by a close of houses.

Note: *If you plan to stay overnight at Canterbury's youth hostel, do not veer left here but continue ahead and maintain direction as far as the A2050 New Dover Road. Cross with care and turn left. The youth hostel is set beside this road at number 54 (☎ 01227 462911).*

The tarmac path leads to a residential area where you walk ahead to a T-junction, then turn right, crossing a railway bridge and curving left. When the houses end maintain direction on a narrow metalled lane between hedges – a route shared with the Elham Valley Way.[1] Near the head of the slope pause for a last backward view of Canterbury Cathedral.

Passing a complex of storage buildings wander ahead between arable fields, and maintain direction at minor crossroads. Immediately after passing beneath power cables the lane forks. Take the right branch alongside a little woodland, and at the next junction continue ahead beside a line of windbreak trees. Beyond converted oast houses at **Hode Farm** the lane is flanked by more arable fields, then becomes a typical sunken lane leading to a junction on the outskirts of Patrixbourne (Grid ref: 187555).

Turn left, then right at a mini roundabout to enter **Patrixbourne**.[2] Passing St Mary's Church on your right keep along the road until you reach the first field on the left.

Note: *For accommodation and/or refreshments in **Bridge** remain on the road which leads directly to the village on the far side of the A2.*

The North Downs Way slants across the field to a woodland corner then skirts the headland alongside the wood, now parting company with the Elham Valley Way. Pass a bench seat with views across the valley to Bridge; just beyond this you'll notice another NDW marker stone. In the field corner go through a gate and along an enclosed footpath parallel with the A2. Shortly after crossing a farm road go through a gate on the left and cross a field diagonally to another woodland corner where you bear right (Grid ref: 193533).

Maintain direction beyond the wood on the right-hand side of a line

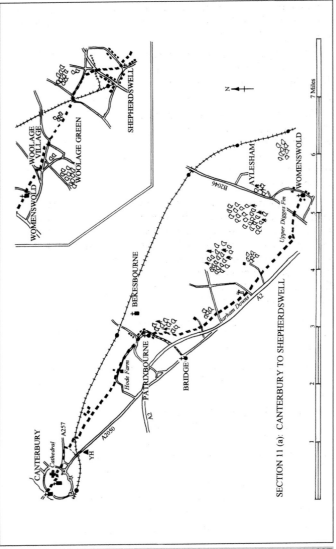

SECTION 11 (a): CANTERBURY TO SHEPHERDSWELL

The lavishly carved south doorway of Patrixbourne Church

of windbreak trees, then cross a minor road and continue through the middle of a very long field on the far side of which you come to a second narrow road. Maintain direction across **Barham Downs**. Keep ahead at another farm road and through more extensive fields where a grass track eventually leads to **Upper Digges Farm**. Here you will come to a crossing track and bear left round the side of the farm to gain a distant view of the cooling towers at Richborough Power Station several miles away to the north-east.

Turn right onto a track by a barn, but leave it when the left-hand hedge ends, to cut across the field corner towards two telegraph poles by the B2046 (Grid ref: 222509). Cross the road with care to a bridleway going ahead between fields, and so come to **Womenswold** (*accommodation, refreshments*) near the church of St Margaret of Antioch which stands on a mound just to the right. Go slightly left ahead to a continuing track, and just beyond a house turn left through a gap, then immediately go to the right along the headland of a field.

On reaching a road pause for a moment to enjoy the view back to Womenswold, then cross the road and walk through a belt of woodland to a second road. Follow this to the right for about 100 yards, then cross a stile on the left by a children's play area. Now wander along the right headland of a field a little to the north of **Woolage Village**. Near the end of the fence-line a stile on the right gives access to the village green where you bear left to another stile. Crossing this turn right and walk round the field edge parallel with a country road.

Near the bottom corner go onto the road and maintain direction until it curves left. At this point go ahead on a track which soon forks. Continue up a slope between hedges, and progress alongside a wood. At the end of a long tree-lined stretch the path edges a field to join a track curving right. This leads to a minor road by a railway bridge (Grid ref: 254492).

Cross the bridge and turn right into Long Lane. Shortly after passing Long Lane Farm take a grass track on the right, passing a cottage and eventually coming out at a T-junction of roads on the edge of **Shepherdswell**. Turn right, and over a level crossing on the line of the East Kent Light Railway, go through a gate on the left to a grass area. The path leads to a NDW noticeboard by a gate. Continue ahead on a track between bungalows and into a field. Maintain direction to a second field which you enter by a stile, and go up the slope to a track reached by another stile. This leads past stables, out through a kissing gate and ahead between houses to a road near the church of St Andrew.

Note: *For refreshments and accommodation turn right here. Shepherdswell also has a station on the Canterbury–Dover line.*

Items of interest:

1: The Elham Valley Way is a 23 mile (37km) waymarked route between Canterbury and Hythe devised and developed by Kent County Council. The Elham Valley itself is a lovely, gentle one, funnelling through rich downland scenery dotted with unspoilt villages. See *Elham Valley Way* by Brian Hart (Kent County Council).

2: Patrixbourne has several fine half-timbered houses, and the

*One of several interesting houses beside the
North Downs Way in Patrixbourne*

Norman church of St Mary with a magnificently carved South
doorway (second in splendour only to Barfreston's). The carvings here
are thought to have been created by the masons who worked on
Rochester Cathedral and Barfreston Church. Bifrons Park no longer
has its mansion (seat of the Marquis Conyngham), although several
village houses betray the fact that they once belonged to the estate.

SECTION 12(a): SHEPHERDSWELL TO DOVER

Distance:	**8 miles (12½km)**
Maps:	**Harveys North Downs Way East 1:40,000**
	OS Landranger 179 Canterbury & East Kent 1:50,000
	OS Explorer 138 Dover, Folkestone & Hythe 1:25,000
Accommodation:	**Dover**
Refreshments:	**Pubs at Minacre (+ ½ mile) and Ashley (+ ½ mile), and Dover**

The final stage of the North Downs Way takes the walk through the continuing agricultural landscape of the open Downs, with pockets of woodland and a section of parkland, but no real villages actually on the route. It is only near the very end, as you approach Dover, that the folding nature of the North Downs reasserts itself. The sparkle of the English Channel is a seductive lure as you wander south with the formidable outline of Dover Castle standing abrupt against the skyline shortly before you plunge down the final slope into the town for a well-deserved rest.

An enclosed footpath takes the North Downs Way out of Shepherdswell alongside the churchyard to a field. Walk down the left headland, but in a short distance cross a stile to enter the next field to the left and maintain direction down its right-hand boundary. In the bottom corner go through a gap into a large open field which you cross half-left ahead, and then maintain direction over the next field you come to.

Both these fields had been recently ploughed and the path had not yet been reinstated. Since the previous days had been particularly wet, the prospect of crossing was not one to be viewed with pleasure – as it proved. The going was now very

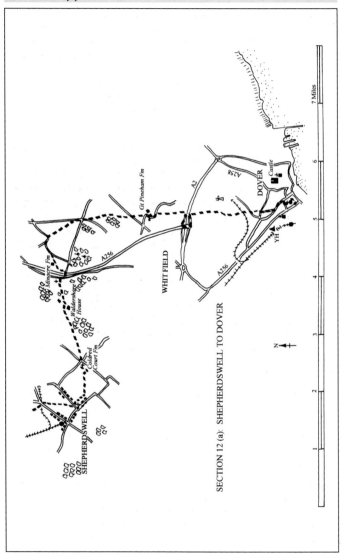

SECTION 12 (a): SHEPHERDSWELL TO DOVER

heavy indeed, and the weight of my boots increased tenfold as huge glutinous discs of mud clung to them as I staggered across the furrows like a drunken astronaut. And when at last the sanctuary of grass was gained, I spent a good five minutes prising the mud off with a stick in a savage mood – until, that is, the walk resumed with birds singing, a welcome burst of sunshine set the damp grass steaming, and my spirits rose once more. In such ways the mood of the long distance walker is thrown from one extreme to the other.

On the far side of the second field go through a gap in the hedge which disguises the line of a dismantled railway, and cross another field to a stile giving access to a meadow below **Coldred Court Farm**. Cut across a paddock in front of the farm to the top left-hand corner to reach a country lane by the tiny church of St Pancras.[1] Turn right, and at minor crossroads cross to a woodland corner and wander through on a footpath leading to a narrow strip of field. This is crossed to more woods with a brick-built water tower in view to the right.

Go through the woods and emerge into a very large field which has to be crossed to the left-hand end of a woodland seen in the distance. On reaching this a stile gives access into Waldershare Park. Veer slightly left ahead, passing in front of the impressive **Waldershare House**[2] to another stile, and maintain direction among mature parkland trees.[3] In the bottom corner come onto a metalled drive near the main gates of the house, and follow this when it curves left towards Home Farm.

Pass through a gateway and bear right, but at a four-way crossing of drives walk ahead by a noticeboard to a stile giving access to a meadow where the path makes for a cicular grove of trees. The way passes through the grove and out the other side where you maintain direction to more trees, then enter the overgrown churchyard of All Saints, Waldershare[4] (Grid ref: 297483).

Leave by the lychgate and walk down the gravel drive to a road, then turn right. (The OS map is in error here.) On coming to a T-junction soon after bear left to cross the A256, then left again on a drive to **Minacre Farm**. Just before reaching the farm cross a stile on the right and aim for to the top left-hand corner of a field where you come to a farm track. Enter the field on the left of the track and walk up the slope aiming for the right-hand end of a row of trees. There you will find a gap in the hedge giving onto a minor road. Bear left into **Ashley**, which forms part of the parish of Sutton.

When the road forks take the right-hand option, and when it makes a sharp left-hand bend, turn right into North Downs Close, then branch left to enter fields. A grass track carries the North Downs Way between fields, but on coming to a high iron stile, cross and maintain direction to a country lane. The English Channel can now be seen far off to the left. Turn right on the Roman road and go ahead at crossroads in the direction of Whitfield and Dover (Grid ref: 314476).

As the road curves slightly to the right, take the path ahead between fields, in effect continuing the line of the original Roman road. The North Downs Way here shares the route of the White Cliffs Country Trail. On coming to a junction of paths continue ahead, now between fences, then alongside a woodland where a final NDW milestone announces 3 miles to Dover. Beyond the woodland the path strikes up through a field to another road.

Cross to a footpath in a tunnel of trees leading to Pineham, then walk ahead on a road which soon curves round and between the buildings of **Great Pineham Farm**. At the next left-hand bend leave the road in favour of a grass track between fences.

On reaching the busy A2 veer right up a sliproad to cross the main road, then bear left down another sliproad on the south side to regain the North Downs Way where a signpost directs the route over a stile and along another enclosed footpath. As the way progresses, so you gain a first view of Dover Castle ahead as if to confirm that the end of the walk is in sight. Descending a slope the path leads to a narrow lane, crosses a railway bridge and continues downhill beside Charlton Cemetery on the outskirts of **Dover**. Coming to a T-junction cross directly ahead to a metalled path rising between high banks leading to Connaught Road. Cross half-left ahead into Park Avenue, which you follow as far as a multi-road junction. Bear left along Maison Dieu Road, but then turn right into Pencaster Road by Dover Magistrates Court. Passing a bus station enter a park on the left, and cross this to Church Street. With the church now on your right, go along King Street to the Market Square to complete your walk along the North Downs Way (Grid ref: 319414).

Note: *For youth hostel accommodation, leave the Market Square by heading left to the A256. Turn right to reach London Road (still the A256).* **Dover Youth Hostel** *is number 306; it stands on the left-hand side of the road (☎ 01304 201314).*

DOVER (*accommodation, refreshments*) has all services, including railway to Canterbury, Ashford and London, and no shortage of accommodation, including a youth hostel. Noted mainly as Britain's premier ferry port, the town is nonetheless a historic one. It was defended by Iron Age man, and the Romans were deterred from landing here by a crowd of well-armed locals. However, having made landfall at Richborough, the Romans chose Dover as the site for their town, *Dubris*, and built two lighthouses here in the 1st century to guide shipping to the harbour. One of these lighthouses (or *pharos*) remains standing today. Among the more recent sites of interest in the town is a memorial to Captain Webb, first man to swim the Channel in 1875, and in North Fall Meadow near the castle, the granite outline of a simple plane marks the spot where, on 25 July 1909, Louis Bleriot landed after making the first powered flight across the Channel. (Tourist Information Centre: Burlington House, Townwall St, Dover CT16 1JR ☎ 01304 205108.)

Items of interest:
1: The church of St Pancras, Coldred stands in a large earthwork which rims two sides of the churchyard.

2: Waldershare House is a large brick Queen Anne mansion built in the early 18th century for Sir Henry Furnese who bought the estate in 1705, but died seven years later as the house was nearing completion.

3: The trees of Waldershare Park were enhanced by the legacy of Miss Mary Hornby (1910–1990), 'a great lover of trees and a Maid of Kent'. Following the devastation of the storm of October 1987, the Men of the Trees planted 1237 saplings, a mixture of hedgerow, forest and ornamental trees in an attempt to rehabilitate part of the Park.

The elegant frontage of Waldershare House, a Queen Anne mansion beside the North Downs Way

4: All Saints, Waldershare was declared redundant in 1981. Inside, it is the 17th and 18th century monuments, housed in two red-brick chapels, that hold your attention, that of Sir Henry Furnese being huge.

APPENDIX A: USEFUL ADDRESSES

1: Countryside Agency
   South-East Regional Office
   71 Kingsway LONDON WC2B 6ST

2: North Downs Way Manager
   Kent County Council
   Environmental Management Unit
   Strategic Planning Directorate
   Invicta House
   County Hall
   MAIDSTONE
   Kent ME14 1XX (☎ 01622 221526)

3: Public Rights of Way Manager (Kent County Council)
   Stategic Planning Directorate
   Invicta House
   County Hall
   MAIDSTONE
   Kent ME14 1XX (☎ 01622 221513)

4: Public Rights of Way Manager (Surrey County Council)
   Environmental Department
   County Hall
   KINGSTON UPON THAMES
   Surrey KT1 2DN (☎ 0208 5419331)

5: The Ramblers' Association
   1/5 Wandsworth Road
   LONDON SW8 2XX (☎ 020 7339 8500)

6: South-East England Tourist Board
   The Old Brew House
   Warwick Park
   TUNBRIDGE WELLS
   Kent TN2 5TU (☎ 01892 540766)

7: Youth Hostels Association (England & Wales)
   8 St Stephen's Hill
   ST ALBANS
   Herts AL1 2DY (☎ 0870 870 8808)

8: Stilwell Publishing Ltd
   59 Charlotte Road
   Shoreditch
   LONDON EC2A 3QT (☎ 020 7739 7179)

APPENDIX B: PUBLIC TRANSPORT INFORMATION

1: Connex South Eastern Trains
   (Serving stations on or near NDW between Dunton Green and Dover)
   Timetable info (☎ 0845 748 4950)

2: Kent Public Transport Section
   Gibson Drive
   Kings Hill
   WEST MALLING
   Kent ME19 4DQ (☎ Freephone 08457 696996)

3: Surrey Public Transport Group
   Highways & Transportation Department
   Surrey County Council
   County Hall
   KINGSTON UPON THAMES
   Surrey KT1 2DN (Travel-line ☎ 01737 223000)

4: Connex South Central Trains
   (Serving stations on or near NDW from Farnham to Oxted)
   Timetable info (☎ 0845 748 4950)

5: Thames Trains
   (Serving stations on or near NDW from Guildford to Redhill)
   Timetable info (☎ 0845 748 4950)

APPENDIX C: RECOMMENDED READING

Allen, D	*Discovering the North Downs Way* (Shire Publications)
Belloc, H	*The Old Road* (Constable)
Bignall, A	*The Kent Village Book* (Countryside Books)
Castle, A	*Long Distance Paths, South-East England* (A & C Black)
Charles, A	*Exploring the Pilgrims Way* (Countryside Books)
Collins, M (ed)	*On Foot Through History* (Oxford Illustrated Press)
Curtis, N & Walker, J	*North Downs Way* (Aurum Press)
Hall, D	*English Medieval Pilgrimages* (Routledge)
Major, A	*Hidden Kent* (Countryside Books)
Mason, O	*South-East England* (Bartholomew)
Reynolds, K	*Classic Walks in Southern England* (Oxford Illustrated Press)
	Visitors Guide to Kent (Moorland Publishing)
	Walking in Kent, Vols I & II (Cicerone Press)
Sands, H	*Memorials of Old Kent*
Scholes, R	*Understanding the Countryside* (Moorland Publishing)
Spence, K	*Companion Guide to Kent & Sussex* (Collins)
Wright, CJ	*Guide to the Pilgrims Way and North Downs Way* (Constable)

CICERONE GUIDES

THE MIDLANDS

CANAL WALKS Vol: 2 Midlands   *Dennis Needham*
  ISBN 1 85284 225 3 176pp

TWENTY COTSWOLD TOWNS   *Clive Holmes*
  Clive describes and draws the most interesting features of these attractive towns.
  ISBN 1 85284 249 0 144pp A4 Case bound

THE COTSWOLD WAY   *Kev Reynolds*
  A glorious walk of 102 miles along high scarp edges, through woodlands and magical villages by
  one of Britain's best guide writers.
  ISBN 1 85284 049 8 168pp

COTSWOLD WALKS (3 volumes)   *Clive Holmes*
  60 walks of between 1 and 10 miles, with local points of interest explained. Beautifully illustrated.
  ISBN 1 85284 139 7 (North) 144pp
  ISBN 1 85284 140 0 (Central) 160pp
  ISBN 1 85284 141 9 (South) 144pp

THE GRAND UNION CANAL WALK   *Clive Holmes*
  13 easy stages along the canal which links the Black Country to London. Delightful illustrations.
  ISBN 1 85284 206 7 128pp

AN OXBRIDGE WALK   *J.A. Lyons*
  Over 100 miles linking the university cities of Oxford and Cambridge. Generally undemanding and
  easy to follow.
  ISBN 1 85284 166 4 168pp

WALKING IN OXFORDSHIRE   *Leslie Tomlinson*
  36 walks from all parts of the county, and suitable for all the family.
  ISBN 1 85284 244 X 200pp

WALKING IN WARWICKSHIRE   *Brian Conduit*
  Attractive pastoral and gentle hill walks include Shakespeare country, the Avon and the Stour.
  Features many historic villages.
  ISBN 1 85284 255 5 136pp

WALKING IN WORCESTERSHIRE   *David Hunter*
  Part of the ever growing County Series, this book describes walks for all the family in
  Worcestershire.
  ISBN 1 85284 286 5 200pp 9

WEST MIDLANDS ROCK   *Doug Kerr*
  A guide to the popular crags.
  ISBN 1 85284 200 8 168pp

SOUTH AND SOUTH-WEST LONG DISTANCE TRAILS

THE KENNET & AVON WALK   *Ray Quinlan*
  90 miles along riverside and canal, from Westminster to Avonmouth, full of history, wildlife, delectable villages and pubs.
  ISBN 1 85284 090 0 200pp

THE LEA VALLEY WALK   *Leigh Hatts*
  Split into 20 stages this 50 mile walk is one of the finest and most varied walking routes around the
  capital, tracing the route of the River Lea from the Millennium Dome to its source.
  ISBN 1 85284 313 6 128pp

THE SOUTH DOWNS WAY
Kev Reynolds

A glorious easterly walk from Eastbourne. The routes are each split into 12 day sections, with advice on stopping points.

THE SOUTHERN COAST-TO-COAST WALK
Ray Quinlan

The equivalent of the popular northern walk. 283 miles from Weston-super-Mare to Dover.
ISBN 1 85284 117 6 200pp

SOUTH WEST WAY - A Walker's Guide to the Coast Path
Martin Collins
Vol.1: Minehead to Penzance
ISBN 1 85284 025 0 184pp PVC cover

Vol.2: Penzance to Poole
ISBN 1 85284 026 9 198pp PVC cover

Two volumes which cover the spectacular 560 mile coastal path around Britain's south-west peninsula. Profusely illustrated and filled with practical details.

THE THAMES PATH
Leigh Hatts

From the Thames Barrier to the source. This popular guide provides all the information needed to complete this delightful scenic route. 180 miles in 20 stages.
ISBN 1 85284 270 9 184pp

THE TWO MOORS WAY
James Roberts

100 miles crossing Dartmoor the delightful villages of central Devon and Exmoor to the rugged coast at Lynmouth.
ISBN 1 85284 159 1 100pp £5.99

THE WEALDWAY AND THE VANGUARD WAY
Kev Reynolds

Two long distance walks, from the outskirts of London to the south coast. The 81 mile Wealdway runs from Gravesend to Beachy Head, while the 62 mile Vanguard Way goes from Croydon to Seaford Head in Sussex.
ISBN 0 902363 85 9 160pp

SOUTHERN AND SOUTH-EAST ENGLAND

CANAL WALKS Vol 3: South
Dennis Needham
ISBN 1 85284 227 X 176pp

WALKING IN BEDFORDSHIRE
Alan Castle

32 fascinating walks of short and medium length for all abilities and interests. Maps and details of local interest abound.
ISBN 1 85284 312 8

WALKING IN BUCKINGHAMSHIRE
Robert Wilson

32 walks through bluebell woods, rolling Chiltern hills and pretty villages. The walks are of short and medium length for all abilities and interests, including sections of Icknield Way.
ISBN 1 85284 301 2

WALKING IN THE CHILTERNS
Duncan Unsworth

35 short circular walks in this area of woods and little valleys with cosy pubs and old churches.
ISBN 1 85284 127 3 184pp

WALKING IN HAMPSHIRE
David Foster and Nick Chandler

With a range of landscapes from coastal beaches and marsh, downlands, river valleys and the New Forest, this county offers exceptional beauty. Delightful walks of short and medium length.
ISBN 1 85284 311 X

A WALKER'S GUIDE TO THE ISLE OF WIGHT *Martin Collins & Norman Birch*
The best walks on this sunshine island, including short circuits and longer trails.
ISBN 1 85284 221 0 216 pp

WALKING IN KENT: Vol I *Kev Reynolds*
ISBN 1 85284 192 3 200pp

WALKING IN KENT: Vol II *Kev Reynolds*
ISBN 1 85284 156 7 200pp
Two books which cover the best of walking in the county.

LONDON THEME WALKS *Frank Duerden*
Ten fascinating walks based on popular themes.
ISBN 1 85284 145 1 144pp

RURAL RIDES No.1: WEST SURREY
ISBN 1 85284 272 5 192pp

RURAL RIDES No.2: EAST SURREY *Ron Strutt*
ISBN 1 85284 273 3 160pp

WALKING IN SUSSEX *Kev Reynolds*
40 walks in the great variety of scenery and history of Sussex. Short walks and more demanding routes, including outline descriptions of some of the region's long distance paths.
ISBN 1 85284 292 X 240pp

SOUTH-WEST ENGLAND

CHANNEL ISLAND WALKS *Paddy Dillon*
47 one-day walks in this wonderful holiday area, with easy bus and boat services. Walks on Jersey, Guernsey, Alderney, Sark and Herm.
ISBN 1 85284 288 1

CORNISH ROCK *Rowland Edwards & Tim Dennell*
A superb photo topo guide to West Penwith, the most popular climbing in Cornwall, by the area's leading activists.
ISBN 1 85284 208 3 234pp A5 size Casebound

WALKING IN CORNWALL *John Earle*
30 walks including the Coast Path and the interesting interior.
ISBN 1 85284 217 2 200pp

WALKING ON DARTMOOR *John Earle*
The most comprehensive walking guide to the National Park. Includes 43 walks and outlines 4 longer walks.
ISBN 0 902363 84 0 224pp

WALKING IN DEVON *David Woodthorpe*
16 coastal, 15 countryside and 14 Dartmoor walks.
ISBN 1 85284 223 7 200pp

WALKING IN DORSET *James Roberts*
Circular walks between 5 and 12 miles in a rich variety of scene. Spectacular coastline, lovely downs and fine pubs.
ISBN 1 85284 180 X 232pp

A WALKER'S GUIDE TO THE PUBS OF DARTMOOR
Chris Wilson & Michael Bennie
60 Dartmoor inns. Everything a walker needs to know.
ISBN 1 85284 115 X 152 pp

EXMOOR AND THE QUANTOCKS   *John Earle*
   Walks for all the family on the moors, valleys and coastline.
   ISBN 1 85284 083 8 200pp

WALKING IN THE ISLES OF SCILLY   *Paddy Dillon*
   With its mild climate and relaxing atmosphere, this is an ideal retreat. Walks and boat trips are
   described, with stunning scenery and beautiful plants and flowers.
   ISBN 1 85284 310 1

WALKING IN SOMERSET   *James Roberts*
   Walks between 3 and 12 miles, gentle rambles to strenuous hikes, on Exmoor, the Quantocks and
   the pastoral lowlands.
   ISBN 1 85284 253 9 280pp

NORTHERN ENGLAND LONG DISTANCE TRAILS

WALKING THE CLEVELAND WAY AND THE MISSING LINK   *Malcolm Boyes*
   Britain's 2nd LD path, the 115 mile circular tour of the North York Moors, including some of our
   finest coastline.
   ISBN 1 85284 014 5 144pp

THE DALES WAY   *Terry Marsh*
   A practical handbook to a very popular walk. An ideal introduction to LD walking. Gentle, pictur-
   esque with accommodation guide.
   ISBN 1 85284 102 8 136pp

THE ISLE OF MAN COASTAL PATH   *Aileen Evans*
   The coastline is of exceptional beauty. The Raad ny Foillan path encircles the island; the Herring Way
   and Millennium Way are also described.
   ISBN 1 85284 277 6 152pp

THE ALTERNATIVE PENNINE WAY   *Denis Brook & Phil Hinchliffe*
   The APW goes from Ashbourne in Derbyshire to Jedburgh in the Borders, 431 km. Milder and more
   pleasant than the PW.
   ISBN 1 85284 095 1 272pp

THE PENNINE WAY   *Martin Collins*
   By popular demand, Cicerone has produced a guide to the Pennine Way. Thoroughly researched by
   one of our most expert authors, this gives everything you need to know about Britain's first LD Trail.
   ISBN 1 85284 262 8 144pp

THE ALTERNATIVE COAST TO COAST   *Denis Brook & Phil Hinchliffe*
   From Walney Island on the edge of the Lake District to Holy Island in Northumberland, across some
   of Britain's finest hill country.
   ISBN 1 85284 202 4 272pp

A NORTHERN COAST TO COAST WALK   *Terry Marsh*
   The most popular LD walk in Britain, from St Bees to Robin Hood's Bay. Includes accommodation
   guide.
   ISBN 1 85284 126 5 280pp

LAKE DISTRICT AND MORECAMBE BAY

A LAKE DISTRICT ANGLER'S GUIDE   *Laurence Tetley*
   Following his successful guide for anglers in Yorkshire the author gives full details for fishing in the
   Lake District. Clubs, shops, permits etc. - an indispensable guide.
   ISBN 1 85284 283 0 248pp

THE CUMBRIA WAY AND ALLERDALE RAMBLE
Jim Watson

A guide to two popular Lake District long distance walks done in Jim's inimitable style. Includes the 75 mile Cumbria Way from Carlisle to Ulverston, and the 50 mile Allerdale Ramble from Seathwaite north-west to Grune Point.
ISBN 1 85284 242 3

THE EDEN WAY
Charlie Emett

A walk through part of Cumbria, following the R. Eden from Carlisle to Kirkby Stephen. Can be broken into sections by using the Settle-Carlisle railway.
ISBN 1 85284 040 4 192pp

CONISTON COPPER MINES: A Field Guide
Eric G. Holland

For mine explorers and the visitor or hill walker.
ISBN 0 902363 36 0 120pp

SHORT WALKS IN LAKELAND
Aileen & Brian Evans

Book 1: SOUTH LAKELAND *ISBN 1 85284 144 3 328pp*
Book 2: NORTH LAKELAND *ISBN 1 85284 232 6 328pp*
Book 3: WEST LAKELAND *ISBN 1 85284.308 X*
Around 60 walks in each book, on the lower fells and dales, described, mapped and illustrated in detail. Highly acclaimed. Book 2 was OWG/COLA Best Guidebook 1997

SCRAMBLES IN THE LAKE DISTRICT
R.B. Evans

ISBN 0 902363 39 5 192pp PVC cover

MORE SCRAMBLES IN THE LAKE DISTRICT
R.B. Evans

ISBN 1 85284 042 0 200p PVC cover
Exciting rock scrambles in gills or up crags to thrill the mountaineer.

SOUTH LAKELAND CYCLE RIDES
Jennifer Richards

21 circular cycle routes for all the family. Graded from easy to challenging, using quiet roads and tracks.
ISBN 1 85284 294 6

THE TARNS OF LAKELAND VOL I: WEST
John & Anne Nuttall

ISBN 1 85284 171 0 240pp

THE TARNS OF LAKELAND VOL 2: EAST
John & Anne Nuttall

Lakeland Book of the Year prize winner 1996. Walks to delectable tarns. Illustrated with superb drawings.
ISBN 1 85284 210 5 200pp

WALKING ROUND THE LAKES
John & Anne Nuttall

The ideal walk encompassing all the major summits, yet with high and low level alternatives. 145 miles in 15 stages.
ISBN 1 85284 099 4 240pp

WALKS IN THE SILVERDALE/ARNSIDE AONB
R.B. Evans

A well-illustrated guide to short walks in this delightful area on the fringe of the Lake District. Fully revised.
ISBN 0 902363 78 6 168pp

WINTER CLIMBS IN THE LAKE DISTRICT
Bob Bennett, Bill Birkett, Brian Davison

Packed with the latest routes which confirm the area as a major winter climbing venue when conditions allow.
ISBN 1 85284 246 6 200pp PVC

NORTH-WEST ENGLAND

WALKING IN CHESHIRE   *Carl Rogers*
  30 walks to suit all abilities in this diverse landscape.
  ISBN 1 85284 153 2 140pp

FAMILY WALKS IN THE FOREST OF BOWLAND   *Jack Keighley*
  30 walks written and illustrated in the author's unique manner.
  ISBN 1 85284 251 2 72pp Wire bound

WALKING IN THE FOREST OF BOWLAND   *Gladys Sellers*
  Despite the limited access in this AONB moorland area, these 30 beautiful walks take best advantage
  of the area. Packed with history and good maps.
  ISBN 1 85284 154 0 168pp

CANAL WALKS, Vol 1: North   *Dennis Needham*
  A guide to some short walks following the canal network.
  ISBN 1 85284 148 6 176pp

LANCASTER CANAL WALKS   *Mary Welsh*
  A guide to circular walks based on the canal, beautifully illustrated by Christine Isherwood.
  ISBN 1 85284 138 9 120pp A5

A WALKER'S GUIDE TO THE LANCASTER CANAL   *Robert Swain*
  Preston to Kendal, including the branch to Glasson Dock, together with the fascinating history of
  the canal.
  ISBN 1 85284 055 2 124pp

WALKS FROM THE LEEDS-LIVERPOOL CANAL   *Mary Welsh*
  34 circular walks based on the canal. Illustrated by Christine Isherwood's superb drawings.
  ISBN 1 85284 212 1 144pp

THE RIBBLE WAY   *Gladys Sellers*
  This 70 mile walk from sea to source close to a junction with the Pennine Way.
  ISBN 1 85284 107 9 112pp

WALKS IN RIBBLE COUNTRY   *Jack Keighley*
  30 family walks, with maps and diagrams all beautifully drawn.
  ISBN 1 85284 284 9 72pp   spiral binding.

WALKING IN LANCASHIRE   *Mary Welsh*
  39 walks described on a seasonal basis. Illustrated superbly by David Macaulay and Linda Waters.
  ISBN 1 85284 191 5 160pp A5 size

WALKS ON THE WEST PENNINE MOORS
  A companion guide to the recreation area   *Gladys Sellers*
  A guide to the popular Lancashire Pennines. 40 short walks, and suggestions for 4 longer walks.
  ISBN 0 902363 92 1 192pp

WALKS IN LANCASHIRE WITCH COUNTRY   *Jack Keighley*
  30 family walks with maps and diagrams all beautifully drawn.
  ISBN 1 85284 093 5 72pp spiral binding.